# THE NEW FOLGER
## SHAKESPE

D0451423

Designed to make Shakespeare's great plays available to all readers, the New Folger Library edition of Shakespeare's plays provides accurate texts in modern spelling and punctuation, as well as scene-by-scene action summaries, full explanatory notes, many pictures clarifying Shakespeare's language, and notes recording all significant departures from the early printed versions. Each play is prefaced by a brief introduction, by a guide to reading Shakespeare's language, and by accounts of his life and theater. Each play is followed by an annotated list of further readings and by a "Modern Perspective" written by an expert on that particular play.

Barbara A. Mowat was Director of Research *emerita* at the Folger Shakespeare Library, Consulting Editor of *Shakespeare Quarterly,* and author of *The Dramaturgy of Shakespeare's Romances* and of essays on Shakespeare's plays and their editing.

Paul Werstine is Professor of English at the Graduate School and at King's University College at Western University. He is a general editor of the New Variorum Shakespeare and author of *Early Modern Playhouse Manuscripts and the Editing of Shakespeare* and of many papers and articles on the printing and editing of Shakespeare's plays.

# The Folger Shakespeare Library

The Folger Shakespeare Library in Washington, D.C., a privately funded research library dedicated to Shakespeare and the civilization of early modern Europe, was founded in 1932 by Henry Clay and Emily Jordan Folger, and incorporated as part of Amherst College in Amherst, Massachusetts, one of the nation's oldest liberal arts colleges, from which Henry Folger had graduated in 1879. In addition to its role as the world's preeminent Shakespeare collection and its emergence as a leading center for Renaissance studies, the Folger Shakespeare Library offers a wide array of cultural and educational programs and services for the general public.

EDITORS

BARBARA A. MOWAT
*Former Director of Research emerita*
*Folger Shakespeare Library*

PAUL WERSTINE
*Professor of English*
*King's University College*
*at Western University, Canada*

**Folger SHAKESPEARE LIBRARY**

By
**WILLIAM SHAKESPEARE**

Edited by Barbara A. Mowat
and Paul Werstine

**Simon & Schuster Paperbacks**
New York  London  Toronto  Sydney  New Delhi

Simon & Schuster
1230 Avenue of the Americas
New York, NY 10020

This Simon & Schuster trade paperback edition May 2020

SIMON & SCHUSTER and colophon are registered trademarks of Simon & Schuster, Inc.

For information about special discounts for bulk purchases, please contact Simon & Schuster Special Sales at 1-866-506-1949 or business@simonandschuster.com.

The Simon & Schuster Speakers Bureau can bring authors to your live event. For more information or to book an event, contact the Simon & Schuster Speakers Bureau at 1-866-248-3049 or visit our website at www.simonspeakers.com.

10  9  8  7  6  5  4  3  2  1

ISBN 978-1-9821-5690-9
ISBN 978-1-5011-2656-7 (ebook)

# From the Director of the Folger Shakespeare Library

It is hard to imagine a world without Shakespeare. Since their composition more than four hundred years ago, Shakespeare's plays and poems have traveled the globe, inviting those who see and read his works to make them their own.

Readers of the New Folger Editions are part of this ongoing process of "taking up Shakespeare," finding our own thoughts and feelings in language that strikes us as old or unusual and, for that very reason, new. We still struggle to keep up with a writer who could think a mile a minute, whose words paint pictures that shift like clouds. These expertly edited texts, presented here with accompanying explanatory notes and up-to-date critical essays, are distinctive because of what they do: they allow readers not simply to keep up, but to engage deeply with a writer whose works invite us to think, and think again.

These New Folger Editions of Shakespeare's plays are also special because of where they come from. The Folger Shakespeare Library in Washington, D.C., where the Editions are produced, is the single greatest documentary source of Shakespeare's works. An unparalleled collection of early modern books, manuscripts, and artwork connected to Shakespeare, the Folger's holdings have been consulted extensively in the preparation of these texts. The Editions also reflect the expertise gained through the regular performance of Shakespeare's works in the Folger's Elizabethan Theatre.

I want to express my deep thanks to editors Barbara Mowat and Paul Werstine for creating these indispensable editions of Shakespeare's works, which incorporate the best of textual scholarship with a richness of commentary that is both inspired and engaging. Readers who want to know more about Shakespeare and his plays can follow the paths these distinguished scholars have trod by visiting the Folger itself, where a range of physical and digital resources (available online) exists to supplement the material in these texts. I commend to you these words, and hope that they inspire.

*Michael Witmore*
Director, Folger Shakespeare Library

# Contents

# Editors' Preface

In recent years, ways of dealing with Shakespeare's texts and with the interpretation of his plays have been undergoing significant change. This edition, while retaining many of the features that have always made the Folger Shakespeare so attractive to the general reader, at the same time reflects these current ways of thinking about Shakespeare. For example, modern readers, actors, and teachers have become interested in the differences between, on the one hand, the early forms in which Shakespeare's plays were first published and, on the other hand, the forms in which editors through the centuries have presented them. In response to this interest, we have based our edition on what we consider the best early printed version of a particular play (explaining our rationale in a section called "An Introduction to This Text") and have marked our changes in the text—unobtrusively, we hope, but in such a way that the curious reader can be aware that a change has been made and can consult the "Textual Notes" to discover what appeared in the early printed version.

Current ways of looking at the plays are reflected in our brief prefaces, in many of the commentary notes, in the annotated lists of "Further Reading," and especially in each play's "Modern Perspective," an essay written by an outstanding scholar who brings to the reader his or her fresh assessment of the play in the light of today's interests and concerns.

As in the Folger Library General Reader's Shakespeare, which this edition replaces, we include explanatory notes designed to help make Shakespeare's language clearer to a modern reader, and we place the notes on the page facing the text that they explain. We also follow the earlier edition in including illustrations —of objects, of clothing, of mythological figures—from books and manuscripts in the Folger Library collection. We provide fresh accounts of the life of Shakespeare, of the publishing of his plays, and of the theaters in which his plays were performed, as well as an introduction to the text itself. We also include a section called "Reading Shakespeare's Language," in which we try to help readers learn to "break the code" of Elizabethan poetic language.

For each section of each volume, we are indebted to a host of generous experts and fellow scholars. The "Reading Shakespeare's Language" sections, for example, could not have been written had not Arthur King, of Brigham Young University, and Randal Robinson, author of *Unlocking Shakespeare's Language,* led the way in untangling Shakespearean language puzzles and generously shared their insights and methodologies with us. "Shakespeare's Life" profited by the careful reading given it by S. Schoenbaum, "Shakespeare's Theater" was read and strengthened by Andrew Gurr and John Astington, and "The Publication of Shakespeare's Plays" is indebted to the comments of Peter W. M. Blayney. We, as editors, take sole responsibility for any errors in our editions.

We are grateful to the authors of the "Modern Perspectives"; to Leeds Barroll and David Bevington for their generous encouragement; to the Huntington and Newberry Libraries for fellowship support; to King's College for the grants it has provided to Paul Werstine; to the Social Sciences and Humanities Research Council of Canada, which provided him with a Research Time Stipend for 1990–91; to R. J. Shroyer of the University of Western Ontario for essential computer support; and to the Folger Institute's Center for Shakespeare Studies for its fortuitous sponsorship of a workshop on "Shakespeare's Texts for Students and Teachers" (funded by the National Endowment for the Humanities and led by Richard Knowles of the University of Wisconsin), a workshop from which we learned an enormous amount about what is wanted by college and high-school teachers of Shakespeare today.

Our biggest debt is to the Folger Shakespeare Library —to Werner Gundersheimer, Director of the Library, who made possible our edition; to Deborah Curren-Aquino, who provides extensive editorial and production support; to Jean Miller, the Library's Art Curator, who combs the Library holdings for illustrations, and to Julie Ainsworth, Head of the Photography Department, who carefully photographs them; to Peggy O'Brien, former Director of Education at the Folger and now Director of Education Programs at the Corporation for Public Broadcasting, and her assistant at the Folger, Molly Haws, who gave us expert advice about the needs being expressed by Shakespeare teachers and students (and to Martha Christian and other "master teachers" who used our texts in manuscript in their classrooms); to Jessica Hymowitz, who provides expert computer support; to the staff of the Academic Programs Division, especially Amy Adler, Mary Tonkinson, Lena Cowen Orlin, Linda Johnson, Kathleen Lynch, and Carol Brobeck; and, finally, to the staff of the Library Reading Room, whose patience and support are invaluable.

Barbara A. Mowat and Paul Werstine

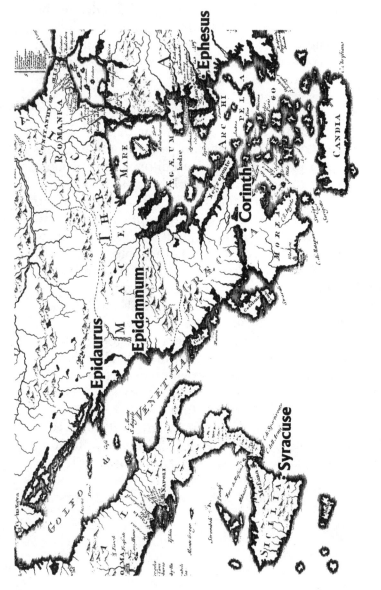

A map of the Mediterranean, with Ephesus, Syracuse, and Corinth.
From Cornelis de Bruyn, *A voyage to the Levant . . .* (1702).

# Shakespeare's
## *The Comedy of Errors*

Shakespeare's lively *Comedy of Errors*, widely agreed to be the slapstick farce of his youth, begins in a most unexpected way—as a nightmare. It introduces its audience to the old merchant Egeon, who lost his wife and one of his sons many years before, and who has been painfully searching for his other son for five years. As the play opens, the old man has just entered the city of Ephesus to continue the search, only to find himself immediately arrested and sentenced to death—not because he has committed a crime, but just because he is a Syracusan in Ephesus, a city whose relations with Syracuse have soured during the old man's five-year quest. Egeon has for so long been distressed by the dispersal and loss of his family that he almost welcomes his own death, which he expects to come at the end of the day.

The gloom of Egeon's suffering lifts after the first scene as the play catches us up in a swirl of events and becomes the farce of "errors," or mistaken identifications, that its title promises us. The notion of farce carries with it a helpful cooking analogy in the verb "to farce," which means to stuff a bird for roasting. Before we get very far into *The Comedy of Errors*, we find it as full of laughable complications as any bird was ever full of stuffing.

Shakespeare started off with a classical source, Plautus's *Menaechmi*, a play about a pair of identical twins who, unknown to each other, find themselves in the same city after a lifetime apart, to their own confusion and to the confusion of all who know one but not the other. In the tradition of farce, Shakespeare then set out to multiply the opportunities for comic misidentification by stuffing into his play not one pair of twins but two, giving the twin Antipholuses twin servants, the Dromios. Borrowing from another play by Plautus, *Amphitruo*, Shakespeare has the wife of one Antipholus entertain the other Antipholus while her husband is locked out of his own house. He also gives one of the servants a memorably obese and lustful fiancée, whose attentions terrify the servant's mystified twin brother. As each Antipholus meets the other's Dromio and then his own Dromio, over and then over again, the play becomes so crammed with misunderstandings, with growing resentments, and with anxieties that we are hard-pressed to keep in mind that this "comedy of errors" carries within it rather simple solutions to its tangled questions. When the confusions lead to arrests for unpaid debts and to exorcisms for demonic possession, we begin to doubt that the play can be wound up in comic resolution, especially a resolution that includes the threatened old Egeon, who returns at the end for his appointment with the executioner, long after most of us have forgotten all about him.

Perhaps the most spirited character in this farce is Adriana, the wife of one of the Antipholuses. The play endows her with language rich in imagery and passionate in tone, language that explores her resentment at being under the domination of a husband who seems not to respect her, combined with devotion to the welfare and success of that very husband. In the conflicted speeches of Adriana, in some of Antipholus of Syracuse's reflections, and in other places worth looking for, Shakespeare suggests complexities beyond the mere complications of farce.

After you have read the play, we invite you to turn to the essay printed after it, *"The Comedy of Errors:* A Modern Perspective," written by Professor Arthur F. Kinney of the University of Massachusetts.

# Reading Shakespeare's Language: *The Comedy of Errors*

For many people today, reading Shakespeare's language can be a problem—but it is a problem that can be solved. Those who have studied Latin (or even French or German or Spanish) and those who are used to reading poetry will have little difficulty understanding the language of Shakespeare's poetic drama. Others, though, need to develop the skills of untangling unusual sentence structures and of recognizing and understanding poetic compressions, omissions, and wordplay. And even those skilled in reading unusual sentence structures may have occasional trouble with Shakespeare's words. Four hundred years of "static" intervene between his speaking and our hearing. Most of his immense vocabulary is still in use, but a few of his words are not, and, worse, some of his words now have meanings quite different from those they had in the sixteenth century. In the theater, most of these difficulties are solved for us by actors who study the language and articulate it for us so that the essential meaning is heard—or, when combined with stage action, is at least *felt.* When reading on one's own, one must do what each actor does: go over the lines (often with a dictionary close at hand) until the puzzles are solved and the lines yield up their poetry and the characters speak in words and phrases that are, suddenly, rewarding and wonderfully memorable.

## Shakespeare's Words

As you begin to read the opening scenes of a play by Shakespeare, you may notice occasional unfamiliar words. Some are unfamiliar simply because we no longer use them. In the opening scenes of *The Comedy of Errors*, for example, you will find the words *embracements* (i.e., embraces), *plainings* (i.e., crying), *hap* (i.e., good fortune), and *defeatures* (i.e., marred features). Words of this kind are explained in notes to the text and will become familiar the more of Shakespeare's plays you read.

In *The Comedy of Errors*, as in all of Shakespeare's writing, more problematic are the words that we still use but that we use with a different meaning. In the opening scenes of *The Comedy of Errors*, for example, the word *wanting* has the meaning of "lacking," *default* is used where we would say "offense," *heavier* is used where we would say "more sorrowful," *happy* where we would say "fortunate," and *doubtful* where we would say "dreadful." Such words will be explained in the notes to the text, and they, too, will become familiar as you continue to read Shakespeare's language.

Some words are strange not because of the "static" introduced by changes in language over the past centuries but because these are words that Shakespeare is using to build a dramatic world that has its own space, time, and history. In the opening scene of *The Comedy of Errors*, for example, Shakespeare creates a world of violence and harsh judicial punishment with such words as *fall* (i.e., death, destruction), *doom* (i.e., judgment, sentence), *outrage* (i.e., violence), *mortal and intestine jars* (i.e., deadly conflicts); and then, in Egeon's story, a world of sea trade and shipwrecks, with words like *deep* (i.e., ocean), *small spare mast* (i.e., a piece of timber for a jury-rigged mast), with such nautical terminology as *making amain* (i.e., coming at full speed) and *borne upon* (i.e., thrust upon by the wind), and with references to *factors* (i.e., agents) and *goods at random left* (i.e., goods left untended). The language of the play's second scene creates the city of Ephesus as a center of commerce and trade with such words as *the mart* (i.e., the open marketplace), *o'erraught* (i.e., cheated), *cozenage* (i.e., deception, fraud) and as a city famous for witchcraft and sorcery/trickery with references to *sorcerers, witches, jugglers,* and *prating mountebanks.*

## Shakespeare's Sentences

In an English sentence, meaning is quite dependent on the place given each word. "The dog bit the boy" and "The boy bit the dog" mean very different things although the individual words are the same. Because English places such importance on the positions of words in sentences, on the way words are arranged, unusual arrangements can puzzle a reader. Shakespeare frequently shifts his sentences away from "normal" English arrangements—often to create the rhythm he seeks, sometimes to use a line's poetic rhythm to emphasize a particular word, sometimes to give a character his or her own speech patterns or to allow the character to speak in a special way. When we attend a good performance of the play, the actors will have worked out the sentence structures and will articulate the sentences so that the meaning is clear. In reading for yourself, do as the actor does. That is, when you become puzzled by a character's speech, check to see if words are being presented in an unusual sequence.

Look first for the placement of subject and verb. Shakespeare often rearranges verbs and subjects (e.g., instead of "He goes" we find "Goes he," or instead of "I would go" we find "Would I go"). In *The Comedy of Errors*, when Egeon says "There *had she not been* long," he is using such a construction. Shakespeare also frequently places the object or the predicate adjective before the subject and verb (e.g., instead of "I hit him" we might find "Him I hit," or instead of "It is black" we might find "Black it is"). Egeon's "*Those*, for their parents were exceeding poor, / *I bought*" is an example of such an inversion, as is his "*A league* from Epidamium *had we sailed.*"

Inversions are not the only unusual sentence structures in Shakespeare's language. Often in his sentences words that would normally appear together are separated from each other. (Again, this is often done to create a particular rhythm or to stress a particular word.) Take, for example, Egeon's "the incessant *weepings of my wife*, / Weeping before for what she saw must come, / *And* piteous *plainings of the pretty babes*, / That mourned for fashion, ignorant what to fear, / *Forced me to seek delays* for them and me." Here, the compound subject ("weepings of my wife" and "plainings of the pretty babes") is separated from the predicate ("Forced me to seek delays") first by a line of description about the wife ("Weeping before for what she saw must come") and then by a line about the crying babies ("That mourned for fashion, ignorant what to fear"). Or take the Duke's lines: "*Hapless Egeon*, whom the fates have marked / To bear the extremity of dire mishap, / Now, trust me, *were it not against our laws,* / Against my crown, my oath, my dignity, / Which princes, would they, may not disannul, / *My soul should sue as advocate for thee."* Here, the "normal" construction "Hapless Egeon, were it not against our laws, my soul should sue as advocate for thee" is interrupted by the insertion of several parenthetical phrases and clauses. In order to create for yourself sentences that seem more like the English of everyday speech, you may wish to rearrange the words, putting together the word clusters (e.g., "the incessant weepings of my wife and piteous plainings of the pretty babes forced me to seek delays"). You will usually find that the sentence will gain in clarity but will lose its rhythm or shift its emphasis.

Locating and rearranging words that "belong together" is especially necessary in passages that separate basic sentence elements by long delaying or expanding interruptions. When the Duke tells Egeon the reason why mercy is being withheld ("The enmity which sprung from the rancorous outrage of your duke excludes all pity from our threat'ning looks"), he uses such an interrupted construction:

> *The enmity and discord which of late*
> *Sprung from the rancorous outrage of your duke*
> To merchants, our well-dealing countrymen,
> Who, wanting guilders to redeem their lives,
> Have sealed his rigorous statutes with their bloods,
> *Excludes all pity from our threat'ning looks.*

Embedded within the larger interrupted construction of these lines is a smaller example of such a construction, as the phrase "merchants who have sealed his statutes with their bloods" is itself expanded by two descriptive interrupting phrases.

In many of Shakespeare's plays, sentences are sometimes complicated not because of unusual structures or interruptions but because Shakespeare omits words and parts of words that English sentences normally require. (In conversation, we, too, often omit words. We say "Heard from him yet?" and our hearer supplies the missing "Have you.") Frequent reading of Shakespeare —and of other poets—trains us to supply such missing words. In his later plays, Shakespeare uses omissions both of verbs and of nouns to great dramatic effect. In *The Comedy of Errors* omissions are rare and seem to be used primarily for the sake of speech rhythm. For example, in Egeon's "Yet this my comfort: when your words are done," the omission of the word "is" after "this" allows a regular iambic pentameter line to be created.

## Shakespearean Wordplay

Shakespeare plays with language so often and so variously that entire books are written on the topic. Here we will mention only three kinds of wordplay, puns, metaphors, and similes. A pun is a play on words that sound the same but that have different meanings (or on a single word that has more than one meaning). Much of the farcical comedy of *The Comedy of Errors* depends on puns and related kinds of wordplay. The twin Dromios serve their masters in roles close to that of the professional Fool—that is, they attempt to entertain, amuse, and distract through wordplay. When, for example, Antipholus of Syracuse meets Dromio of Ephesus in 1.2,

Dromio delivers his message to Antipholus in words that involve a series of puns:

> I from my mistress come to you in post;
> If I return, I shall be post indeed,
> For she will scour your fault upon my pate.

Here, "in post" means "in haste" (like a messenger traveling by post-horse); Dromio picks up the word *post* in the next line, giving it the meaning of "the tavern post on which charges for drinks were cut or scored" and then builds on that pun in the following line with a triple pun on the word *scour*, which means "to beat," but which is pronounced like "score" and which, in the phrase "scour your fault," means "purge away (your sin)."

To give only one other example from hundreds available in this play: In 2.2, Antipholus of Syracuse confronts Dromio of Syracuse and orders him to behave properly, "or I will beat this method in your sconce." Dromio replies: "'Sconce' call you it? So you would leave battering, I had rather have it a 'head.' An you use these blows long, I must get a sconce for my head and ensconce it too. . . ." Dromio takes the word *sconce,* which Antipholus has used as a slang term for "head," plays on its meanings as a "fortification" being subjected to *battering* and as a "protective screen," and then adds the word *ensconce,* which means "to shelter behind a fortification." Such wide-ranging puns are so characteristic of the language of this play—particularly the conversations that involve either Dromio—that the play's dialogue needs to be listened to carefully if one is to catch all its meanings.

Metaphors and similes are plays on words in which one object or idea is expressed as if it were something

else, something with which it shares common features.
When Antipholus of Syracuse is left alone onstage in
1.2, he shares with the audience his feelings of being
lost, confused, and unhappy by comparing himself to
a drop of water in the sea looking for another drop,
expanding on the proverb "as lost as a drop of water
in the sea":

> I to the world am like a drop of water
> That in the ocean seeks another drop,
> Who, falling there to find his fellow forth,
> Unseen, inquisitive, confounds himself.
> So I, to find a mother and a brother,
> In quest of them, unhappy, lose myself.

The wordplay here is technically a simile, in that
Antipholus explicitly says that he is *like* a drop of water,
but the comparison becomes metaphoric (i.e., the speak-
er in effect *becomes* the drop of water) with the word
*confounds*, which means "destroys," but which carries
the meaning of its Latin root, *confundere*, "to pour
together." Antipholus's complex emotions are here conveyed quite economically through metaphoric language.

Adriana uses much the same metaphor/simile in 2.2
when she describes to her supposed husband what
marriage means to her:

> Ah, do not tear away thyself from me!
> For know, my love, as easy mayst thou fall
> A drop of water in the breaking gulf,
> And take unmingled thence that drop again
> Without addition or diminishing,
> As take from me thyself and not me too.

Here, the ocean ("the breaking gulf") is the marriage,
Antipholus is the drop of water falling into the ocean;

she argues that once the drop has fallen, it cannot be removed "unmingled." This is only the first of several metaphors/similes used by Adriana to show, for example, that their bodies are one, or that he is the elm tree and she the ivy twined inseparably around the tree. (The fact that she is speaking to the wrong brother makes the situation wonderfully comic, but does not detract from the interest of her language.)

## Implied Stage Action

Finally, in reading Shakespeare's plays we should always remember that what we are reading is a performance script. The dialogue is written to be spoken by actors who, at the same time, are moving, gesturing, picking up objects, weeping, shaking their fists. Some stage action is described in what are called "stage directions"; some is suggested within the dialogue itself. We must learn to be alert to such signals as we stage the play in our imaginations. When, in *The Comedy of Errors* 1.2.8, the merchant says to Antipholus "There is your money that I had to keep" and Antipholus in turn says to Dromio "Go bear it to the Centaur," it is clear that the merchant gives a purse to Antipholus who then gives it to Dromio. In 2.2.184, when Adriana says to Antipholus "Come, I will fasten on this sleeve of thine," it is equally clear that she takes him by the arm. At several places in *The Comedy of Errors*, signals to the reader are not quite so clear. When, for example, Adriana says to Antipholus at 2.2.135 (in a line quoted above) "Ah, do not tear away thyself from me," it is not at all clear when or how she has attached herself to him; nor is it clear, in 3.1, just when the outraged husband and his servant should begin beating on the door. Dromio urges his master to "knock the door hard" at 3.1.89, but dialogue a few lines earlier ("Well struck! There was blow for blow") may refer to verbal blows or to physical blows on the door. As editors, we have added stage directions when we feel reasonably sure our suggestions are valid, but readers, directors, and actors will need to use their own imaginations and their own understandings of the scene for their individual stagings.

Especially interesting challenges are offered by 3.1 and by the final scene of the play. In 3.1, it is unclear where—or whether—the characters "inside the house" should appear when they speak, so that the staging of this scene is one of the most problematic in Shakespeare. In the play's final scene, the interest is primarily in character placement when the two sets of twins are finally onstage together. The miracle of the untangling of the day's confusions is signaled in the Folio text with the stage direction *"All gather to see them"* as the second set of twins enters. Most affected by the entrance are Adriana ("I see two husbands, or mine eyes deceive me") and Egeon (denied by one son, but now hearing the words "Egeon art thou not . . . ?" and "O, my old master.—Who hath bound him here?") These recognitions are then superseded by the Abbess's "Whoever bound him, I will loose his bonds / And gain a husband by his liberty." Proper placement of characters onstage and proper attention to entrances will have a significant effect on the power of the denouement, whether onstage or in our imaginations.

It is immensely rewarding to work carefully with Shakespeare's language so that the words, the sentences, the wordplay, and the implied stage action all become clear—as readers for the past four centuries have discovered. It may be more pleasurable to attend a good performance of a play—though not everyone has thought so. But the joy of being able to stage one of Shakespeare's plays in one's imagination, to return to passages that continue to yield further meanings (or further questions) the more one reads them—these are pleasures that, for many, rival (or at least augment) those of the performed text, and certainly make it worth considerable effort to "break the code" of Elizabethan poetic drama and let free the remarkable language that makes up a Shakespeare text.

# Shakespeare's Life

Surviving documents that give us glimpses into the life of William Shakespeare show us a playwright, poet, and actor who grew up in the market town of Stratford-upon-Avon, spent his professional life in London, and returned to Stratford a wealthy landowner. He was born in April 1564, died in April 1616, and is buried inside the chancel of Holy Trinity Church in Stratford.

We wish we could know more about the life of the world's greatest dramatist. His plays and poems are testaments to his wide reading—especially to his knowledge of Virgil, Ovid, Plutarch, Holinshed's *Chronicles*, and the Bible—and to his mastery of the English language, but we can only speculate about his education. We know that the King's New School in Stratford-upon-Avon was considered excellent. The school was one of the English "grammar schools" established to educate young men, primarily in Latin grammar and literature. As in other schools of the time, students began their studies at the age of four or five in the attached "petty school," and there learned to read and

# CATECHISMVS

*paruus pueris primùm Latinè*
*qui ediscatur, proponendus*
*in Scholis.*

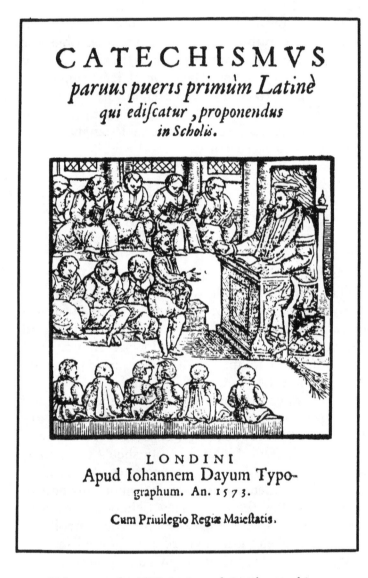

LONDINI
Apud Iohannem Dayum Typo-
graphum. An. 1573.

Cum Priuilegio Regiæ Maieſtatis.

Title page of a 1573 Latin and Greek catechism
for children.

write in English, studying primarily the catechism from the Book of Common Prayer. After two years in the petty school, students entered the lower form (grade) of the grammar school, where they began the serious study of Latin grammar and Latin texts that would occupy most of the remainder of their school days. (Several Latin texts that Shakespeare used repeatedly in writing his plays and poems were texts that schoolboys memorized and recited.) Latin comedies were introduced early in the lower form; in the upper form, which the boys entered at age ten or eleven, students wrote their own Latin orations and declamations, studied Latin historians and rhetoricians, and began the study of Greek using the Greek New Testament.

Since the records of the Stratford "grammar school" do not survive, we cannot prove that William Shakespeare attended the school; however, every indication (his father's position as an alderman and bailiff of Stratford, the playwright's own knowledge of the Latin classics, scenes in the plays that recall grammar-school experiences—for example, *The Merry Wives of Windsor*, 4.1) suggests that he did. We also lack generally accepted documentation about Shakespeare's life after his schooling ended and his professional life in London began. His marriage in 1582 (at age eighteen) to Anne Hathaway and the subsequent births of his daughter Susanna (1583) and the twins Judith and Hamnet (1585) are recorded, but how he supported himself and where he lived are not known. Nor do we know when and why he left Stratford for the London theatrical world, nor how he rose to be the important figure in that world that he had become by the early 1590s.

We do know that by 1592 he had achieved some prominence in London as both an actor and a playwright. In that year was published a book by the playwright Robert Greene attacking an actor who had the audacity to write blank-verse drama and who was "in his own conceit [i.e., opinion] the only Shakescene in a country." Since Greene's attack includes a parody of a line from one of Shakespeare's early plays, there is little doubt that it is Shakespeare to whom he refers, a "Shake-scene" who had aroused Greene's fury by successfully competing with university-educated dramatists like Greene himself. It was in 1593 that Shakespeare became a published poet. In that year he published his long narrative poem *Venus and Adonis;* in 1594, he followed it with *The Rape of Lucrece.* Both poems were dedicated to the young earl of Southampton (Henry Wriothesley), who may have become Shakespeare's patron.

It seems no coincidence that Shakespeare wrote these narrative poems at a time when the theaters were closed because of the plague, a contagious epidemic disease that devastated the population of London. When the theaters reopened in 1594, Shakespeare apparently resumed his double career of actor and playwright and began his long (and seemingly profitable) service as an acting-company shareholder. Records for December 1594 show him to be a leading member of the Lord Chamberlain's Men. It was this company of actors, later named the King's Men, for whom he would be a principal actor, dramatist, and shareholder for the rest of his career.

So far as we can tell, that career spanned about twenty years. In the 1590s, he wrote his plays on English history as well as several comedies and at least two tragedies (*Titus Andronicus* and *Romeo and Juliet*). These histories, comedies, and tragedies are the plays credited to him in 1598 in a work, *Palladis Tamia,* that in one chapter compares English writers with "Greek, Latin,

The Globe

A stylized representation of the Globe theater.
From Claes Jansz Visscher, *Londinum florentissima
Britanniae urbs* . . . (c. 1625).

and Italian Poets." There the author, Francis Meres, claims that Shakespeare is comparable to the Latin dramatists Seneca for tragedy and Plautus for comedy, and calls him "the most excellent in both kinds for the stage." He also names him "Mellifluous and honey-tongued Shakespeare": "I say," writes Meres, "that the Muses would speak with Shakespeare's fine filed phrase, if they would speak English." Since Meres also mentions Shakespeare's "sugared sonnets among his private friends," it is assumed that many of Shakespeare's sonnets (not published until 1609) were also written in the 1590s.

In 1599, Shakespeare's company built a theater for themselves across the river from London, naming it the Globe. The plays that are considered by many to be Shakespeare's major tragedies (*Hamlet, Othello, King Lear*, and *Macbeth*) were written while the company was resident in this theater, as were such comedies as *Twelfth Night* and *Measure for Measure*. Many of Shakespeare's plays were performed at court (both for Queen Elizabeth I and, after her death in 1603, for King James I), some were presented at the Inns of Court (the residences of London's legal societies), and some were doubtless performed in other towns, at the universities, and at great houses when the King's Men went on tour; otherwise, his plays from 1599 to 1608 were, so far as we know, performed only at the Globe. Between 1608 and 1612, Shakespeare wrote several plays—among them *The Winter's Tale* and *The Tempest*—presumably for the company's new indoor Blackfriars theater, though the plays seem to have been performed also at the Globe and at court. Surviving documents describe a performance of *The Winter's Tale* in 1611 at the Globe, for example, and performances of *The Tempest* in 1611 and 1613 at the royal palace of Whitehall.

Shakespeare wrote very little after 1612, the year in which he probably wrote *King Henry VIII.* (It was at a performance of *Henry VIII* in 1613 that the Globe caught fire and burned to the ground.) Sometime between 1610 and 1613 he seems to have returned to live in Stratford-upon-Avon, where he owned a large house and considerable property, and where his wife and his two daughters and their husbands lived. (His son Hamnet had died in 1596.) During his professional years in London, Shakespeare had presumably derived income from the acting company's profits as well as from his own career as an actor, from the sale of his play manuscripts to the acting company, and, after 1599, from his shares as an owner of the Globe. It was presumably that income, carefully invested in land and other property, which made him the wealthy man that surviving documents show him to have become. It is also assumed that William Shakespeare's growing wealth and reputation played some part in inclining the crown, in 1596, to grant John Shakespeare, William's father, the coat of arms that he had so long sought. William Shakespeare died in Stratford on April 23, 1616 (according to the epitaph carved under his bust in Holy Trinity Church) and was buried on April 25. Seven years after his death, his collected plays were published as *Mr. William Shakespeares Comedies, Histories, & Tragedies* (the work now known as the First Folio).

The years in which Shakespeare wrote were among the most exciting in English history. Intellectually, the discovery, translation, and printing of Greek and Roman classics were making available a set of works and world-views that interacted complexly with Christian texts and beliefs. The result was a questioning, a vital intellectual ferment, that provided energy for the period's amazing dramatic and literary output and that fed

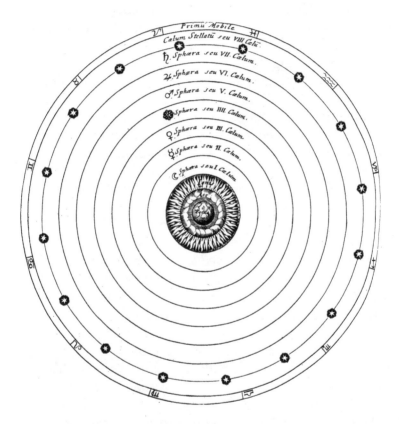

Ptolemaic universe.
From Marcus Manilius, *The sphere of . . .* (1675).

directly into Shakespeare's plays. The Ghost in *Hamlet*, for example, is wonderfully complicated in part because he is a figure from Roman tragedy—the spirit of the dead returning to seek revenge—who at the same time inhabits a Christian hell (or purgatory); Hamlet's description of humankind reflects at one moment the Neoplatonic wonderment at mankind ("What a piece of work is a man!") and, at the next, the Christian disparagement of human sinners ("And yet, to me, what is this quintessence of dust?").

As intellectual horizons expanded, so also did geographical and cosmological horizons. New worlds—both North and South America—were explored, and in them were found human beings who lived and worshiped in ways radically different from those of Renaissance Europeans and Englishmen. The universe during these years also seemed to shift and expand. Copernicus had earlier theorized that the earth was not the center of the cosmos but revolved as a planet around the sun. Galileo's telescope, created in 1609, allowed scientists to see that Copernicus had been correct; the universe was not organized with the earth at the center, nor was it so nicely circumscribed as people had, until that time, thought. In terms of expanding horizons, the impact of these discoveries on people's beliefs—religious, scientific, and philosophical—cannot be overstated.

London, too, rapidly expanded and changed during the years (from the early 1590s to around 1610) that Shakespeare lived there. London—the center of England's government, its economy, its royal court, its overseas trade—was, during these years, becoming an exciting metropolis, drawing to it thousands of new citizens every year. Troubled by overcrowding, by poverty, by recurring epidemics of the plague, London was also a mecca for the wealthy and the aristocratic, and for those who sought advancement at court, or power in government or finance or trade. One hears in Shakespeare's plays the voices of London—the struggles for power, the fear of venereal disease, the language of buying and selling. One hears as well the voices of Stratford-upon-Avon—references to the nearby Forest of Arden, to sheep herding, to small-town gossip, to village fairs and markets. Part of the richness of Shakespeare's work is the influence felt there of the various worlds in which he lived: the world of metropolitan London, the world of small-town and rural England, the world of the theater, and the worlds of craftsmen and shepherds.

That Shakespeare inhabited such worlds we know from surviving London and Stratford documents, as well as from the evidence of the plays and poems themselves. From such records we can sketch the dramatist's life. We know from his works that he was a voracious reader. We know from legal and business documents that he was a multifaceted theater man who became a wealthy landowner. We know a bit about his family life and a fair amount about his legal and financial dealings. Most scholars today depend upon such evidence as they draw their picture of the world's greatest playwright. Such, however, has not always been the case. Until the late eighteenth century, the William Shakespeare who lived in most biographies was the creation of legend and tradition. This was the Shakespeare who was supposedly caught poaching deer at Charlecote, the estate of Sir Thomas Lucy close by Stratford; this was the Shakespeare who fled from Sir Thomas's vengeance and made his way in London by taking care of horses outside a playhouse; this was the Shakespeare who reportedly could barely read but whose natural gifts were extraordinary, whose father was a butcher who allowed his gifted son sometimes to help in the butcher shop, where William supposedly killed calves "in a high style," making a speech for the occasion. It was this legendary William Shakespeare whose Falstaff (in *1* and *2 Henry IV*) so pleased Queen Elizabeth that she demanded a play about Falstaff in love, and demanded that it be written in fourteen days (hence the existence of *The Merry Wives of Windsor*). It was this legendary Shakespeare who reached the top of his acting career in the roles of the Ghost in *Hamlet* and old Adam in *As You Like It*—and who died of a fever contracted by drinking too hard at "a merry meeting" with the poets Michael Drayton and Ben Jonson. This legendary Shakespeare is a rambunctious, undisciplined man, as attractively "wild" as his plays were seen by earlier generations to be. Unfortunately, there is no trace of evidence to support these wonderful stories.

Perhaps in response to the disreputable Shakespeare of legend—or perhaps in response to the fragmentary and, for some, all-too-ordinary Shakespeare documented by surviving records—some people since the mid-nineteenth century have argued that William Shakespeare could not have written the plays that bear his name. These persons have put forward some dozen names as more likely authors, among them Queen Elizabeth, Sir Francis Bacon, Edward de Vere (earl of Oxford), and Christopher Marlowe. Such attempts to find what for these people is a more believable author of the plays is a tribute to the regard in which the plays are held. Unfortunately for their claims, the documents that exist that provide evidence for the facts of Shakespeare's life tie him inextricably to the body of plays and poems that bear his name. Unlikely as it seems to those who want the works to have been written by an aristocrat, a university graduate, or an "important" person, the plays and poems seem clearly to have been produced by a man from Stratford-upon-Avon with a very good "grammar-school" education and a life of experience in London and in the world of the London theater. How this particular man produced the works that dominate the cultures of much of the world almost four hundred years after his death is one of life's mysteries—and one that will continue to tease our imaginations as we continue to delight in his plays and poems.

# Shakespeare's Theater

The actors of Shakespeare's time are known to have performed plays in a great variety of locations. They played at court (that is, in the great halls of such royal residences as Whitehall, Hampton Court, and Greenwich); they played in halls at the universities of Oxford and Cambridge, and at the Inns of Court (the residences in London of the legal societies); and they also played in the private houses of great lords and civic officials. Sometimes acting companies went on tour from London into the provinces, often (but not only) when outbreaks of bubonic plague in the capital forced the closing of theaters to reduce the possibility of contagion in crowded audiences. In the provinces the actors usually staged their plays in churches (until around 1600) or in guildhalls. While surviving records show only a handful of occasions when actors played at inns while on tour, London inns were important playing places up until the 1590s.

The building of theaters in London had begun only shortly before Shakespeare wrote his first plays in the 1590s. These theaters were of two kinds: outdoor or public playhouses that could accommodate large numbers of playgoers, and indoor or private theaters for much smaller audiences. What is usually regarded as the first London outdoor public playhouse was called simply the Theatre. James Burbage—the father of Richard Burbage, who was perhaps the most famous actor in Shakespeare's company—built it in 1576 in an area north of the city of London called Shoreditch. Among the more famous of the other public playhouses that capitalized on the new fashion were the Curtain and the Fortune (both also built north of the city), the Rose, the Swan, the Globe, and the Hope (all located on the Bankside, a region just across the Thames south of the city of London). All these playhouses had to be built outside the jurisdiction of the city of London because many civic officials were hostile to the performance of drama and repeatedly petitioned the royal council to abolish it.

The theaters erected on the Bankside (a region under the authority of the Church of England, whose head was the monarch) shared the neighborhood with houses of prostitution and with the Paris Garden, where the blood sports of bearbaiting and bullbaiting were carried on. There may have been no clear distinction between playhouses and buildings for such sports, for we know that the Hope was used for both plays and baiting and that Philip Henslowe, owner of the Rose and, later, partner in the ownership of the Fortune, was also a partner in a monopoly on baiting. All these forms of entertainment were easily accessible to Londoners by boat across the Thames or over London Bridge.

Evidently Shakespeare's company prospered on the

Bankside. They moved there in 1599. Threatened by difficulties in renewing the lease on the land where their first theater (the Theatre) had been built, Shakespeare's company took advantage of the Christmas holiday in 1598 to dismantle the Theatre and transport its timbers across the Thames to the Bankside, where, in 1599, these timbers were used in the building of the Globe. The weather in late December 1598 is recorded as having been especially harsh. It was so cold that the Thames was "nigh [nearly] frozen," and there was heavy snow. Perhaps the weather aided Shakespeare's company in eluding their landlord, the snow hiding their activity and the freezing of the Thames allowing them to slide the timbers across to the Bankside without paying tolls for repeated trips over London Bridge. Attractive as this narrative is, it remains just as likely that the heavy snow hampered transport of the timbers in wagons through the London streets to the river. It also must be remembered that the Thames was, according to report, only "nigh frozen" and therefore as impassable as it ever was. Whatever the precise circumstances of this fascinating event in English theater history, Shakespeare's company was able to begin playing at their new Globe theater on the Bankside in 1599. After the first Globe burned down in 1613 during the staging of Shakespeare's *Henry VIII* (its thatch roof was set alight by cannon fire called for by the performance), Shakespeare's company immediately rebuilt on the same location. The second Globe seems to have been a grander structure than its predecessor. It remained in use until the beginning of the English Civil War in 1642, when Parliament officially closed the theaters. Soon thereafter it was pulled down.

The public theaters of Shakespeare's time were very different buildings from our theaters today. First of all, they were open-air playhouses. As recent excavations of the Rose and the Globe confirm, some were polygonal or roughly circular in shape; the Fortune, however, was square. The most recent estimates of their size put the diameter of these buildings at 72 feet (the Rose) to 100 feet (the Globe), but we know that they held vast audiences of two or three thousand, who must have been squeezed together quite tightly. Some of these spectators paid extra to sit or stand in the two or three levels of roofed galleries that extended, on the upper levels, all the way around the theater and surrounded an open space. In this space were the stage and, perhaps, the tiring house (what we would call dressing rooms), as well as the so-called yard. In the yard stood the spectators who chose to pay less, the ones whom Hamlet contemptuously called "groundlings." For a roof they had only the sky, and so they were exposed to all kinds of weather. They stood on a floor that was sometimes made of mortar and sometimes of ash mixed with the shells of hazelnuts. The latter provided a porous and therefore dry footing for the crowd, and the shells may have been more comfortable to stand on because they were not as hard as mortar. Availability of shells may not have been a problem if hazelnuts were a favorite food for Shakespeare's audiences to munch on as they watched his plays. Archaeologists who are today unearthing the remains of theaters from this period have discovered quantities of these nutshells on theater sites.

Unlike the yard, the stage itself was covered by a roof. Its ceiling, called "the heavens," is thought to have been elaborately painted to depict the sun, moon, stars, and planets. Just how big the stage was remains hard to determine. We have a single sketch of part of the interior of the Swan. A Dutchman named Johannes de Witt visited this theater around 1596 and sent a sketch of it back to his friend, Arend van Buchel. Because van Buchel found de Witt's letter and sketch of interest, he copied both into a book. It is van Buchel's copy, adapted, it seems, to the shape and size of the page in his book, that survives. In this sketch, the stage appears to be a large rectangular platform that thrusts far out into the yard, perhaps even as far as the center of the circle formed by the surrounding galleries. This drawing, combined with the specifications for the size of the stage in the building contract for the Fortune, has led scholars to conjecture that the stage on which Shakespeare's plays were performed must have measured approximately 43 feet in width and 27 feet in depth, a vast acting area. But the digging up of a large part of the Rose by archaeologists has provided evidence of a quite different stage design. The Rose stage was a platform tapered at the corners and much shallower than what seems to be depicted in the van Buchel sketch. Indeed, its measurements seem to be about 37.5 feet across at its widest point and only 15.5 feet deep. Because the surviving indications of stage size and design differ from each other so much, it is possible that the stages in other theaters, like the Theatre, the Curtain, and the Globe (the outdoor playhouses where we know that Shakespeare's plays were performed), were different from those at both the Swan and the Rose.

After about 1608 Shakespeare's plays were staged not only at the Globe but also at an indoor or private playhouse in Blackfriars. This theater had been constructed in 1596 by James Burbage in an upper hall of a former Dominican priory or monastic house. Although Henry VIII had dissolved all English monasteries in the 1530s (shortly after he had founded the Church of England), the area remained under church, rather than hostile civic, control. The hall that Burbage had purchased and renovated was a large one in which Parliament had once met. In the private theater that he constructed, the stage, lit by candles, was built across the narrow end of the hall, with boxes flanking it. The rest of the hall offered seating room only. Because there was no provision for standing room, the largest audience it could hold was less than a thousand, or about a quarter of what the Globe could accommodate. Admission to Blackfriars was correspondingly more expensive. Instead of a penny to stand in the yard at the Globe, it cost a minimum of sixpence to get into Blackfriars. The best seats at the Globe (in the Lords' Room in the gallery above and behind the stage) cost sixpence; but the boxes flanking the stage at Blackfriars were half a crown, or five times sixpence. Some spectators who were particularly interested in displaying themselves paid even more to sit on stools on the Blackfriars stage.

Whether in the outdoor or indoor playhouses, the stages of Shakespeare's time were different from ours. They were not separated from the audience by the dropping of a curtain between acts and scenes. Therefore the playwrights of the time had to find other ways of signaling to the audience that one scene (to be imagined as occurring in one location at a given time) had ended and the next (to be imagined at perhaps a different location at a later time) had begun. The customary way used by Shakespeare and many of his contemporaries was to have everyone onstage exit at the end of one scene and have one or more different characters enter to begin the next. In a few cases, where characters remain onstage from one scene to another, the dialogue or stage action makes the change of location clear, and the characters are generally to be imagined as having moved from one place to another. For example, in *Romeo and Juliet*, Romeo and his friends remain onstage in Act 1 from scene 4 to scene 5, but they are represented as having moved between scenes from the street that leads to Capulet's house into Capulet's house itself. The new location is signaled in part by the appearance onstage of Capulet's servingmen carrying napkins, something they would not take into the streets. Playwrights had to be quite resourceful in the use of hand properties, like the napkin, or in the use of dialogue to specify where the action was taking place in their plays because, in contrast to most of today's theaters, the playhouses of Shakespeare's time did not use movable scenery to dress the stage and make the setting precise. As another consequence of this difference, however, the playwrights of Shakespeare's time did not have to specify exactly where the action of their plays was set when they did not choose to do so, and much of the action of their plays is tied to no specific place.

Usually Shakespeare's stage is referred to as a "bare stage," to distinguish it from the stages of the last two or three centuries with their elaborate sets. But the stage in Shakespeare's time was not completely bare. Philip Henslowe, owner of the Rose, lists in his inventory of stage properties a rock, three tombs, and two mossy banks. Stage directions in plays of the time also call for such things as thrones (or "states"), banquets (presumably tables with plaster replicas of food on them), and beds and tombs to be pushed onto the stage. Thus the stage often held more than the actors.

The actors did not limit their performing to the stage alone. Occasionally they went beneath the stage, as the Ghost appears to do in the first act of *Hamlet*. From there they could emerge onto the stage through a trapdoor. They could retire behind the hangings across the back of the stage (or the front of the tiring house), as, for example, the actor playing Polonius does when he hides behind the arras. Sometimes the hangings could be drawn back during a performance to "discover" one or more actors behind them. When performance required that an actor appear "above," as when Juliet is imagined to stand at the window of her chamber in the famous and misnamed "balcony scene," then the actor probably climbed the stairs to the gallery over the back of the stage and temporarily shared it with some of the spectators. The stage was also provided with ropes and winches so that actors could descend from, and reascend to, the "heavens."

Perhaps the greatest difference between dramatic performances in Shakespeare's time and ours was that in Shakespeare's England the roles of women were played by boys. (Some of these boys grew up to take male roles in their maturity.) There were no women in the acting companies, only in the audience. It had not always been so in the history of the English stage. There are records of women on English stages in the thirteenth and fourteenth centuries, two hundred years before Shakespeare's plays were performed. After the accession of James I in 1603, the queen of England and her ladies took part in entertainments at court called masques, and with the reopening of the theaters in 1660 at the restoration of Charles II, women again took their place on the public stage.

The chief competitors for the companies of adult actors such as the one to which Shakespeare belonged and for which he wrote were companies of exclusively boy actors. The competition was most intense in the early 1600s. There were then two principal children's companies: the Children of Paul's (the choirboys from St. Paul's Cathedral, whose private playhouse was near the cathedral); and the Children of the Chapel Royal (the choirboys from the monarch's private chapel, who performed at the Blackfriars theater built by Burbage in 1596, which Shakespeare's company had been stopped from using by local residents who objected to crowds). In *Hamlet* Shakespeare writes of "an aerie [nest] of children, little eyases [hawks], that cry out on the top of question and are most tyrannically clapped for 't. These are now the fashion and . . . berattle the common stages [attack the public theaters]." In the long run, the adult actors prevailed. The Children of Paul's dissolved around 1606. By about 1608 the Children of the Chapel Royal had been forced to stop playing at the Blackfriars theater, which was then taken over by the King's Men, Shakespeare's own troupe.

Acting companies and theaters of Shakespeare's time were organized in different ways. For example, Philip Henslowe owned the Rose and leased it to companies of actors, who paid him from their takings. Henslowe would act as manager of these companies, initially paying playwrights for their plays and buying properties, recovering his outlay from the actors. Shakespeare's company, however, managed itself, with the principal actors, Shakespeare among them, having the status of "sharers" and the right to a share in the takings, as well as the responsibility for a part of the expenses. Five of the sharers themselves, Shakespeare among them, owned the Globe. As actor, as sharer in an acting company and in ownership of theaters, and as playwright, Shakespeare was about as involved in the theatrical industry as one could imagine. Although Shakespeare and his fellows prospered, their status under the law was conditional upon the protection of powerful patrons. "Common players"—those who did not have patrons or masters—were classed in the language of the law with "vagabonds and sturdy beggars." So the actors had to secure for themselves the official rank of servants of patrons. Among the patrons under whose protection Shakespeare's company worked were the lord chamberlain and, after the accession of King James in 1603, the king himself.

We are now perhaps on the verge of learning a great deal more about the theaters in which Shakespeare and his contemporaries performed—or at least of opening up new questions about them. Already about 70 percent of the Rose has been excavated, as has about 10 percent of the second Globe, the one built in 1614. It is to be hoped that soon more will be available for study. These are exciting times for students of Shakespeare's stage.

# The Publication of Shakespeare's Plays

Eighteen of Shakespeare's plays found their way into print during the playwright's lifetime, but there is nothing to suggest that he took any interest in their publication. These eighteen appeared separately in editions called quartos. Their pages were not much larger than the one you are now reading, and these little books were sold unbound for a few pence. The earliest of the quartos that still survive were printed in 1594, the year that both *Titus Andronicus* and a version of the play now called *2 King Henry VI* became available. While almost every one of these early quartos displays on its title page the name of the acting company that performed the play, only about half provide the name of the playwright,

Shakespeare. The first quarto edition to bear the name Shakespeare on its title page is *Love's Labor's Lost* of 1598. A few of these quartos were popular with the book-buying public of Shakespeare's lifetime; for example, quarto *Richard II* went through five editions between 1597 and 1615. But most of the quartos were far from best-sellers; *Love's Labor's Lost* (1598), for instance, was not reprinted in quarto until 1631. After Shakespeare's death, two more of his plays appeared in quarto format: *Othello* in 1622 and *The Two Noble Kinsmen*, coauthored with John Fletcher, in 1634.

In 1623, seven years after Shakespeare's death, *Mr. William Shakespeares Comedies, Histories, & Tragedies* was published. This printing offered readers in a single book thirty-six of the thirty-eight plays now thought to have been written by Shakespeare, including eighteen that had never been printed before. And it offered them in a style that was then reserved for serious literature and scholarship. The plays were arranged in double columns on pages nearly a foot high. This large page size is called "folio," as opposed to the smaller "quarto," and the 1623 volume is usually called the Shakespeare First Folio. It is reputed to have sold for the lordly price of a pound. (One copy at the Folger Library is marked fifteen shillings—that is, three-quarters of a pound.)

In a preface to the First Folio entitled "To the great Variety of Readers," two of Shakespeare's former fellow actors in the King's Men, John Heminge and Henry Condell, wrote that they themselves had collected their dead companion's plays. They suggested that they had seen his own papers: "we have scarce received from him a blot in his papers." The title page of the Folio declared that the plays within it had been printed "according to the True Original Copies." Comparing the Folio to the quartos, Heminge and Condell disparaged the quartos, advising their readers that "before you were abused with divers stolen and surreptitious copies, maimed, and deformed by the frauds and stealths of injurious impostors." Many Shakespeareans of the eighteenth and nineteenth centuries believed Heminge and Condell and regarded the Folio plays as superior to anything in the quartos.

Once we begin to examine the Folio plays in detail, it becomes less easy to take at face value the word of Heminge and Condell about the superiority of the Folio texts. For example, of the first nine plays in the Folio (one quarter of the entire collection), four were essentially reprinted from earlier quarto printings that Heminge and Condell had disparaged; and four have now been identified as printed from copies written in the hand of a professional scribe of the 1620s named Ralph Crane; the ninth, *The Comedy of Errors*, was apparently also printed from a manuscript, but one whose origin cannot be readily identified. Evidently then, eight of the first nine plays in the First Folio were not printed, in spite of what the Folio title page announces, "according to the True Original Copies," or Shakespeare's own papers, and the source of the ninth is unknown. Since today's editors have been forced to treat Heminge and Condell's pronouncements with skepticism, they must choose whether to base their own editions upon quartos or the Folio on grounds other than Heminge and Condell's story of where the quarto and Folio versions originated.

Editors have often fashioned their own narratives to explain what lies behind the quartos and Folio. They have said that Heminge and Condell meant to criticize only a few of the early quartos, the ones that offer much shorter and sometimes quite different, often garbled, versions of plays. Among the examples of these are the 1600 quarto of *Henry V* (the Folio offers a much fuller version) or the 1603 *Hamlet* quarto (in 1604 a different, much longer form of the play got into print as a quarto). Early in this century editors speculated that these questionable texts were produced when someone in the audience took notes from the plays' dialogue during performances and then employed "hack poets" to fill out the notes. The poor results were then sold to a publisher and presented in print as Shakespeare's plays. More recently this story has given way to another in which the shorter versions are said to be recreations from memory of Shakespeare's plays by actors who wanted to stage them in the provinces but lacked manuscript copies. Most of the quartos offer much better texts than these so-called bad quartos. Indeed, in most of the quartos we find texts that are at least equal to or better than what is printed in the Folio. Many of this century's Shakespeare enthusiasts have persuaded themselves that most of the quartos were set into type directly from Shakespeare's own papers, although there is nothing on which to base this conclusion except the desire for it to be true. Thus speculation continues about how the Shakespeare plays got to be printed. All that we have are the printed texts.

The book collector who was most successful in bringing together copies of the quartos and the First Folio was Henry Clay Folger, founder of the Folger Shakespeare Library in Washington, D.C. While it is estimated that there survive around the world only about 230 copies of the First Folio, Mr. Folger was able to acquire more than seventy-five copies, as well as a large number of fragments, for the library that bears his name. He also amassed a substantial number of quartos. For example, only fourteen copies of the First Quarto of *Love's Labor's*

*Lost* are known to exist, and three are at the Folger Shakespeare Library. As a consequence of Mr. Folger's labors, twentieth-century scholars visiting the Folger Library have been able to learn a great deal about sixteenth- and seventeenth-century printing and, particularly, about the printing of Shakespeare's plays. And Mr. Folger did not stop at the First Folio, but collected many copies of later editions of Shakespeare, beginning with the Second Folio (1632), the Third (1663–64), and the Fourth (1685). Each of these later folios was based on its immediate predecessor and was edited anonymously. The first editor of Shakespeare whose name we know was Nicholas Rowe, whose first edition came out in 1709. Mr. Folger collected this edition and many, many more by Rowe's successors.

# An Introduction to This Text

*The Comedy of Errors* was first printed in the 1623 collection of Shakespeare's plays now known as the First Folio. The present edition is based directly upon the First Folio version.* For the convenience of the reader, we have modernized the punctuation and the spelling of the Folio. Sometimes we go so far as to modernize certain old forms of words; for example, when *a* means "he," we change it to *he;* we change *mo* to *more* and *ye* to *you.* But it is not our practice in editing any of the plays to modernize words that sound distinctly different from modern forms. For example, when the early printed

---

*We have also consulted the computerized text of the First Folio provided by the Text Archive of the Oxford University Computing Centre, to which we are grateful.

texts read *sith* or *apricocks* or *porpentine*, we have not modernized to *since, apricots, porcupine*. When the forms *an, and,* or *and if* appear instead of the modern form *if*, we have reduced *and* to *an* but have not changed any of these forms to their modern equivalent, *if*. We also modernize and, where necessary, correct passages in foreign languages, unless an error in the early printed text can be reasonably explained as a joke.

Whenever we change the wording of the First Folio or add anything to its stage directions, we mark the change by enclosing it in superior half-brackets (⌐ ¬). We want our readers to be immediately aware when we have intervened. (Only when we correct an obvious typographical error in the First Folio does the change not get marked.) Whenever we change either the First Folio's wording or its punctuation so that the meaning changes, we list the change in the textual notes at the back of the book, even if all we have done is fix an obvious error.

We regularize a number of proper names, as is the usual practice in editions of the play. For example, the Folio sometimes calls Antipholus of Syracuse by the names Antipholis Errotis or Antipholis Erotes in stage directions, but, like other editions, ours refers to this character as Antipholus of Syracuse throughout its text. (For further discussion of these names, see the longer note to 1.2.0 SD, page 165.) The Folio also uses the forms Siracusa and Siracusia, both of which this edition reduces to Syracuse, unless the meter requires the form Syracusa.

This edition differs from many earlier ones in its efforts to aid the reader in imagining the play as a performance rather than as a series of actual events. Thus stage directions are written with reference to the stage. For example, one of the primary ways in which directors help theater audiences keep track of two sets of identically named and costumed twin characters (the Dromios and Antipholuses) is through making prominent the props—the bag of money, the chain, the rope's end, etc.—that each is given at specific points in the play. In our text, therefore, when one Dromio, given a key in 4.1, enters again in 4.2, we add to the Folio stage direction *Enter Dromio* ⌐*of*¬ *Syracuse* the additional information *with the key.* Or, to take another example, Antipholus of Syracuse is given a gold chain in 3.2; in his subsequent entrances, we often add *wearing the chain,* so that readers, like theatergoers, can associate him with earlier action in the play and thereby further differentiate him from his twin, Antipholus of Ephesus. With the addition of such directions, we hope to give our readers a greater opportunity to stage the play in their own imaginations.

For the same reason, whenever we think it is reasonably certain that a speech is accompanied by a particular action, we provide a stage direction describing the action. (Occasional exceptions to this rule occur when the action is so obvious that to add a stage direction would insult the reader.) Stage directions for the entrance of characters in mid-scene are, with rare exceptions, placed so that they immediately precede the characters' participation in the scene, even though these entrances may appear somewhat earlier in the early printed texts. Whenever we move a stage direction, we record this change in the textual notes. Latin stage directions (e.g., *Exeunt)* are translated into English (e.g., *They exit).*

We expand the often severely abbreviated forms of names used as speech headings in early printed texts into the full names of the characters. We also regularize the speakers' names in speech headings, using only a single designation for each character, even though the early printed texts sometimes use a variety of designations. Variations in the speech headings of the early printed texts are recorded in the textual notes.

In the present edition, as well, we mark with a dash any change of address within a speech, unless a stage direction intervenes. When the *-ed* ending of a word is to be pronounced, we mark it with an accent. Like editors for the past two centuries we print metrically linked lines in the following way:

**ANTIPHOLUS OF SYRACUSE**
Thou hast thine own form.
**DROMIO OF SYRACUSE**       No, I am an ape.

However, when there are a number of short verse lines that can be linked in more than one way, we do not, with rare exceptions, indent any of them.

## The Explanatory Notes

The notes that appear on the pages facing the text are designed to provide readers with the help they may need to enjoy the play. Whenever the meaning of a word in the text is not readily accessible in a good contemporary dictionary, we offer the meaning in a note. Sometimes we provide a note even when the relevant meaning is to be found in the dictionary but when the word has acquired since Shakespeare's time other potentially confusing meanings. In our notes, we try to offer modern synonyms for Shakespeare's words. We also try to indicate to the reader the connection between the word in the play and the modern synonym. For example, Shakespeare sometimes uses the word *head* to mean "source," but, for modern readers, there may be no connection evident between these two words. We provide the connection by explaining Shakespeare's usage as follows: **"head:** fountainhead, source.*"* On some occasions, a whole phrase or clause needs explanation. Then, if space allows, we rephrase in our own words the difficult passage, and add at the end synonyms for individual words in the passage. When scholars have been unable to determine the meaning of a word or phrase, we acknowledge the uncertainty.

# THE
# COMEDY
## OF
# ERRORS

# Characters in the Play

EGEON, a merchant from Syracuse
Solinus, DUKE of Ephesus

ANTIPHOLUS OF SYRACUSE, a traveler in search of his
    mother and his brother
DROMIO OF SYRACUSE, Antipholus of Syracuse's
    servant
FIRST MERCHANT, a citizen of Ephesus

ANTIPHOLUS OF EPHESUS, a citizen of Ephesus
DROMIO OF EPHESUS, Antipholus of Ephesus's servant
ADRIANA, Antipholus of Ephesus's wife
LUCIANA, Adriana's sister
LUCE (also called Nell), kitchen maid betrothed to
    Dromio of Ephesus
MESSENGER, servant to Antipholus of Ephesus and
    Adriana

ANGELO, an Ephesian goldsmith
SECOND MERCHANT, a citizen of Ephesus to whom
    Angelo owes money
BALTHASAR, an Ephesian merchant invited to dinner
    by Antipholus of Ephesus
COURTESAN, hostess of Antipholus of Ephesus at
    dinner

DR. PINCH, a schoolmaster, engaged as an exorcist
OFFICER (also called Jailer), an Ephesian law officer

LADY ABBESS (also called Emilia), head of a priory
    in Ephesus

Attendants, Servants to Pinch, Headsman, Officers

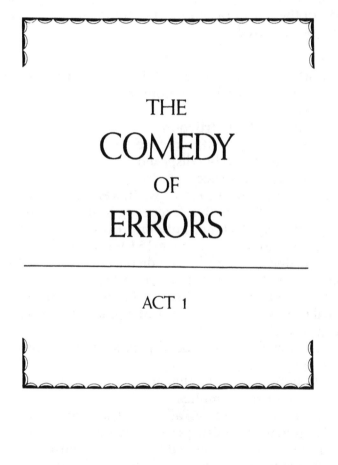

# THE
# COMEDY
## OF
# ERRORS

## ACT 1

**1.1** Egeon, a merchant from Syracuse, is arrested for having illegally entered Ephesus. He tells the story of how he lost his wife and an infant son; the remaining identical-twin son grew up and set out to find his lost brother; Egeon in turn journeyed in search of the son he had raised. His journey has brought him to Ephesus. Now Egeon is given until the end of the day to raise ransom money. If he fails, he will be executed.

---

0 SD. **Ephesus:** a city in Asia Minor; **Syracuse:** a city in Sicily (See longer note, page 163, and map, page xii.)

1. **fall:** death, destruction

2. **doom:** judgment, sentence

4. **partial:** favorably disposed

6. **outrage:** violence

7. **our:** i.e., my (the royal "we"); **well-dealing:** well-behaved, perhaps with reference to business dealings

8. **wanting:** lacking; **guilders:** Dutch or German coins (See longer note, page 163.); **redeem:** ransom

9. **sealed . . . bloods:** i.e., died as the result of his harsh laws (See longer note, page 163.)

10. **Excludes . . . looks:** i.e., the **enmity and discord** (line 5) shown by **your duke** (line 6) prevent me from showing pity to you

11. **mortal . . . jars:** deadly conflicts (See longer note, page 163.)

12. **seditious:** violently partial, turbulent

13. **synods:** assemblies

15. **admit . . . to:** i.e., allow no trade between

17. **marts and fairs:** periodic gatherings of buyers and sellers, often ordained by statute or custom

20. **confiscate:** adjudged forfeited; **dispose:** control, disposal

# ACT 1

---

Scene 1
*Enter ⌜Solinus⌝ the Duke of Ephesus, with ⌜Egeon⌝ the*
*Merchant of Syracuse, Jailer, and other Attendants.*

EGEON
  Proceed, Solinus, to procure my fall,
  And by the doom of death end woes and all.
DUKE
  Merchant of Syracusa, plead no more.
  I am not partial to infringe our laws.
  The enmity and discord which of late                    5
  Sprung from the rancorous outrage of your duke
  To merchants, our well-dealing countrymen,
  Who, wanting guilders to redeem their lives,
  Have sealed his rigorous statutes with their bloods,
  Excludes all pity from our threat'ning looks.           10
  For since the mortal and intestine jars
  'Twixt thy seditious countrymen and us,
  It hath in solemn synods been decreed,
  Both by the Syracusians and ourselves,
  To admit no traffic to our adverse towns.               15
  Nay, more, if any born at Ephesus
  Be seen at Syracusian marts and fairs;
  Again, if any Syracusian born
  Come to the bay of Ephesus, he dies,
  His goods confiscate to the Duke's dispose,              20

7

21. **marks:** See longer note to 1.1.8, page 163.
**levièd:** raised
22. **quit the penalty:** pay the fine
23. **substance:** property, goods; **valued . . . rate:** appraised at the most generous estimate
32. **Than I:** i.e., than for me
33–34. **my end . . . nature:** i.e., my death was caused by my acting according to natural affection
35. **gives me leave:** allows me (to say)
37. **happy:** i.e., fortunate
38. **by me:** i.e., through me as well; **hap:** luck
41. **Epidamium:** i.e., Epidamnus (See longer note, page 163.); **factor's:** agent's
42. **care of:** concern for; **at random:** untended
43. **embracements:** i.e., embraces
45. **herself:** i.e., she herself; **at fainting:** i.e., fainting
46. **pleasing . . . bear:** i.e., pregnancy (See Genesis 3.16, in which God's **punishment** for Eve's disobedience is that women will bear children in pain.)
49. **but:** i.e., before
51–52. **so like . . . As:** i.e., so much like the other that they
52. **but by names:** i.e., except by their names (See longer note, pages 163–64.)

Unless a thousand marks be levièd
To quit the penalty and to ransom him.
Thy substance, valued at the highest rate,
Cannot amount unto a hundred marks;
Therefore by law thou art condemned to die.        25

EGEON
Yet this my comfort: when your words are done,
My woes end likewise with the evening sun.

DUKE
Well, Syracusian, say in brief the cause
Why thou departedst from thy native home
And for what cause thou cam'st to Ephesus.        30

EGEON
A heavier task could not have been imposed
Than I to speak my griefs unspeakable;
Yet, that the world may witness that my end
Was wrought by nature, not by vile offense,
I'll utter what my sorrow gives me leave.        35
In Syracusa was I born, and wed
Unto a woman happy but for me,
And by me, had not our hap been bad.
With her I lived in joy. Our wealth increased
By prosperous voyages I often made        40
To Epidamium, till my factor's death
And ⌜the⌝ great care of goods at random left
Drew me from kind embracements of my spouse;
From whom my absence was not six months old
Before herself—almost at fainting under        45
The pleasing punishment that women bear—
Had made provision for her following me
And soon and safe arrivèd where I was.
There had she not been long but she became
A joyful mother of two goodly sons,        50
And, which was strange, the one so like the other
As could not be distinguished but by names.

54. **mean woman:** i.e., woman of low birth
55. **such a burden:** i.e., a similar birth; **male:** Some editors have heard wordplay on *mail* as "baggage, or burden."
57. **attend:** wait on, serve
58. **not meanly:** i.e., very (literally, not moderately)
59. **Made . . . return:** i.e., urged every day that we return home   **motions:** urgings, proposals
63. **deep:** sea
64. **instance:** sign
68. **doubtful warrant:** dreadful guarantee
71. **before:** in advance
72. **plainings:** i.e., crying
73. **for fashion:** perhaps, as a mere outward action or form; **ignorant . . . fear:** not knowing what they should be afraid of
74. **delays:** postponements (of our **immediate death,** line 68)
75. **this:** i.e., this is the way; **other . . . none:** i.e., there were no other means available
76. **sought . . . boat:** i.e., fled in the ship's rowboat
77. **sinking-ripe:** i.e., about to sink
78. **careful:** anxious; **latter-born:** the twin who was born second
79. **small spare mast:** probably a "yard" or piece of timber used to jury-rig a mast in case of a storm (See longer note, page 164.)
82. **like:** similarly
83. **thus disposed:** i.e., with one twin son and one infant servant attached to each end of the mast
84–85. **Fixing . . . mast:** i.e., each tied ourselves to the end of the mast opposite the baby on whom

*(continued)*

That very hour, and in the selfsame inn,
A mean woman was deliverèd
Of such a burden, male twins, both alike.                     55
Those, for their parents were exceeding poor,
I bought and brought up to attend my sons.
My wife, not meanly proud of two such boys,
Made daily motions for our home return.
Unwilling, I agreed. Alas, too soon                           60
We came aboard.
A league from Epidamium had we sailed
Before the always-wind-obeying deep
Gave any tragic instance of our harm;
But longer did we not retain much hope,                       65
For what obscurèd light the heavens did grant
Did but convey unto our fearful minds
A doubtful warrant of immediate death,
Which though myself would gladly have embraced,
Yet the incessant weepings of my wife,                        70
Weeping before for what she saw must come,
And piteous plainings of the pretty babes,
That mourned for fashion, ignorant what to fear,
Forced me to seek delays for them and me.
And this it was, for other means was none:                    75
The sailors sought for safety by our boat
And left the ship, then sinking-ripe, to us.
My wife, more careful for the latter-born,
Had fastened him unto a small spare mast,
Such as seafaring men provide for storms.                     80
To him one of the other twins was bound,
Whilst I had been like heedful of the other.
The children thus disposed, my wife and I,
Fixing our eyes on whom our care was fixed,
Fastened ourselves at either end the mast                     85
And, floating straight, obedient to the stream,
Was carried towards Corinth, as we thought.

**our eyes,** and **our care,** were **fixed** (This reading would explain how, when the mast was split, the father was left with the younger son, the mother with the elder. See line 124.)

86. **straight:** at once; **stream:** sea current
89. **vapors:** clouds; **offended:** assailed
90. **benefit:** kindness, favor; **his wished:** i.e., the sun's wished-for
92. **from far:** in the distance; **making amain:** coming at full speed
93. **Of Corinth . . . this:** i.e., one from Corinth, one from Epidaurus
95. **Gather the sequel:** i.e., infer what followed; **by that:** i.e., from what
98. **done so:** i.e., pitied me
99. **Worthily termed:** justly called
100. **ere . . . leagues:** i.e., while the ships were still more than ten leagues apart
102. **borne upon:** i.e., thrust upon by the wind (a nautical phrase)
103. **Our helpful ship:** i.e., the mast carrying us; **splitted in the midst:** i.e., split in two
104. **us:** i.e., my wife and me
106. **What . . . what:** i.e., something . . . something
107. **part:** i.e., part of the mast; **seeming as:** i.e., appearing to be, apparently
111. **as we thought:** i.e., as best we could tell
115. **reft:** deprived; **their prey:** i.e., the wife and babies
116. **their bark:** i.e., the ship that **seized on us**
119. **That:** i.e., how

At length the sun, gazing upon the earth,
Dispersed those vapors that offended us,
And by the benefit of his wished light                    90
The seas waxed calm, and we discoverèd
Two ships from far, making amain to us,
Of Corinth that, of Epidaurus this.
But ere they came—O, let me say no more!
Gather the sequel by that went before.                    95
DUKE
Nay, forward, old man. Do not break off so,
For we may pity though not pardon thee.
EGEON
O, had the gods done so, I had not now
Worthily termed them merciless to us.
For, ere the ships could meet by twice five leagues,      100
We were encountered by a mighty rock,
Which being violently borne ⌈upon,⌉
Our helpful ship was splitted in the midst;
So that, in this unjust divorce of us,
Fortune had left to both of us alike                      105
What to delight in, what to sorrow for.
Her part, poor soul, seeming as burdenèd
With lesser weight, but not with lesser woe,
Was carried with more speed before the wind,
And in our sight they three were taken up                 110
By fishermen of Corinth, as we thought.
At length, another ship had seized on us
And, knowing whom it was their hap to save,
Gave healthful welcome to their shipwracked guests,
And would have reft the fishers of their prey             115
Had not their ⌈bark⌉ been very slow of sail;
And therefore homeward did they bend their course.
Thus have you heard me severed from my bliss,
That by misfortunes was my life prolonged
To tell sad stories of my own mishaps.                    120

122. **dilate:** describe, relate
123. **have befall'n of:** has happened to
124. **youngest:** See note to lines 84–85. **care:** object of concern
127. **so . . . like:** i.e., who was in the same situation
128. **Reft:** bereft; **retained:** kept (See longer note to 1.1.52, pages 163–64.)
129. **quest of him:** i.e., search for the other Antipholus
130. **Whom . . . see:** i.e., while yearning or striving to see him (my lost son) **labored of:** This phrase carries the meanings of "being burdened by or suffering under" and "struggling to bring forth, as in childbirth."
131. **whom:** i.e., he whom
133. **bounds of Asia:** See longer note to 1.1.132–34, pages 164–65.
134. **coasting homeward:** i.e., sailing toward home along the coast, or from port to port
135. **Hopeless to find:** i.e., without hope of finding (my son); **unsought:** unexplored
136. **Or . . . or:** i.e., either . . . or
138. **timely:** early; or, perhaps, opportune
143. **dignity:** high position or office
144. **would they:** i.e., even if they wanted to; **disannul:** annul, abolish
145. **sue:** plead
146. **adjudgèd:** sentenced
151. **beneficial:** beneficent

DUKE
And for the sake of them thou sorrowest for,
Do me the favor to dilate at full
What have befall'n of them and ⌐thee¬ till now.

EGEON
My youngest boy, and yet my eldest care,
At eighteen years became inquisitive                    125
After his brother, and importuned me
That his attendant—so his case was like,
Reft of his brother, but retained his name—
Might bear him company in the quest of him,
Whom whilst I labored of a love to see,                 130
I hazarded the loss of whom I loved.
Five summers have I spent in farthest Greece,
Roaming clean through the bounds of Asia,
And, coasting homeward, came to Ephesus,
Hopeless to find, yet loath to leave unsought            135
Or that or any place that harbors men.
But here must end the story of my life;
And happy were I in my timely death
Could all my travels warrant me they live.

DUKE
Hapless Egeon, whom the fates have marked              140
To bear the extremity of dire mishap,
Now, trust me, were it not against our laws,
Against my crown, my oath, my dignity,
Which princes, would they, may not disannul,
My soul should sue as advocate for thee.               145
But though thou art adjudgèd to the death,
And passèd sentence may not be recalled
But to our honor's great disparagement,
Yet will I favor thee in what I can.
Therefore, merchant, I'll limit thee this day          150
To seek thy ⌐life¬ by beneficial help.
Try all the friends thou hast in Ephesus;
Beg thou, or borrow, to make up the sum,

158. **procrastinate:** delay, postpone

**1.2** Antipholus of Syracuse lands in Ephesus with his servant, Dromio. He sends Dromio to an inn with their luggage and money. Antipholus, warned that Syracusans are not allowed in Ephesus, speaks of his search for his mother and his brother. He meets Dromio of Ephesus, who denies having been entrusted with any money and who scolds him for being late coming home to his wife to dinner. Antipholus beats him and sets out for the inn to find his money.

---

0 SD. **Antipholus of Syracuse:** See longer note, page 165.
  1. **give out:** announce, proclaim
  2. **confiscate:** adjudged forfeited
  4. **arrival:** i.e., landing
  9. **the Centaur:** the name of an inn; **host:** lodge
  11. **dinnertime:** i.e., time for the midday meal
  12. **manners:** social conditions, ways of behavior
  15. **travel:** Spelled "trauaile" in the Folio, this word could mean both **travel** and "travail"—i.e., "hardship" or "physical labor."
  18. **a mean:** an opportunity

And live. If no, then thou art doomed to die.—
Jailer, take him to thy custody.                                    155
JAILER   I will, my lord.
EGEON
Hopeless and helpless doth Egeon wend,
But to procrastinate his lifeless end.

                                            *They exit.*


⌐Scene 2⌐
*Enter Antipholus* ⌐*of Syracuse, First*⌐ *Merchant, and*
*Dromio* ⌐*of Syracuse.*⌐

⌐FIRST⌐ MERCHANT
Therefore give out you are of Epidamium,
Lest that your goods too soon be confiscate.
This very day a Syracusian merchant
Is apprehended for arrival here
And, not being able to buy out his life,                            5
According to the statute of the town
Dies ere the weary sun set in the west.
There is your money that I had to keep.
                          ⌐*He gives money.*⌐
ANTIPHOLUS ⌐OF SYRACUSE, *handing money to Dromio*⌐
Go bear it to the Centaur, where we host,
And stay there, Dromio, till I come to thee.                        10
Within this hour it will be dinnertime.
Till that, I'll view the manners of the town,
Peruse the traders, gaze upon the buildings,
And then return and sleep within mine inn,
For with long travel I am stiff and weary.                          15
Get thee away.
DROMIO ⌐OF SYRACUSE⌐
Many a man would take you at your word
And go indeed, having so good a mean.
                    *Dromio* ⌐*of Syracuse*⌐ *exits.*

19. **villain:** servant, social inferior, scoundrel (The word could be used as a term of affection.)
21. **humor:** mood, disposition
22. **What:** an interjection introducing a question
25. **benefit:** profit
26. **Soon at:** i.e., about
27. **Please you:** i.e., if you please (a polite phrase); **upon the mart:** in the marketplace
28. **consort you:** i.e., keep you company
32. **commend . . . content:** i.e., deliver you over to your own pleasures
34. **the thing I cannot get:** Antipholus seems to give **content** the meaning of "contented condition, satisfaction."
35. **to the world:** perhaps, in relation to the world
37. **Who:** i.e., which; **find . . . forth:** This phrase combines the actions of finding and drawing forth. **his fellow:** i.e., its companion
38. **confounds:** destroys (from the Latin *confundere,* which means "to pour together"); **himself:** i.e., itself
40. **unhappy:** (1) unfortunate; (2) sad; **lose myself:** Proverbial: "As lost as a drop of water in the sea."
41. **almanac of my true date:** Like an **almanac** or calendar (see page 52), Dromio reminds Antipholus of his exact age because they were born at the same time. (Antipholus's words are true even though this is the "wrong" Dromio.)
42. **How chance:** i.e., how does it happen

ANTIPHOLUS ⌜OF SYRACUSE⌝
A trusty villain, sir, that very oft,
When I am dull with care and melancholy,                    20
Lightens my humor with his merry jests.
What, will you walk with me about the town
And then go to my inn and dine with me?
⌜FIRST⌝ MERCHANT
I am invited, sir, to certain merchants,
Of whom I hope to make much benefit.                        25
I crave your pardon. Soon at five o'clock,
Please you, I'll meet with you upon the mart
And afterward consort you till bedtime.
My present business calls me from you now.
ANTIPHOLUS ⌜OF SYRACUSE⌝
Farewell till then. I will go lose myself                   30
And wander up and down to view the city.
⌜FIRST⌝ MERCHANT
Sir, I commend you to your own content. ⌜*He exits.*⌝
ANTIPHOLUS ⌜OF SYRACUSE⌝
He that commends me to mine own content
Commends me to the thing I cannot get.
I to the world am like a drop of water                      35
That in the ocean seeks another drop,
Who, falling there to find his fellow forth,
Unseen, inquisitive, confounds himself.
So I, to find a mother and a brother,
In quest of them, unhappy, lose myself.                     40

*Enter Dromio of Ephesus.*

Here comes the almanac of my true date.—
What now? How chance thou art returned so soon?
DROMIO OF EPHESUS
Returned so soon? Rather approached too late!
The capon burns; the pig falls from the spit;
The clock hath strucken twelve upon the bell;              45
My mistress made it one upon my cheek.

47. **hot:** angry

49. **stomach:** appetite

52. **default:** offense (The words **fast, pray, penitent,** and **default** construct Antipholus's being late to dinner as a sin for which others are performing the penance.)

53. **Stop in your wind:** i.e., shut up (literally, close in your breath, as in a stoppered vessel)

56. **crupper:** leather strap that goes under the horse's tail to steady the saddle (See page 66.)

61. **charge:** responsibility; **from:** i.e., out of

63. **in post:** i.e., in haste (like a messenger traveling by post-horse)

64. **post:** i.e., the tavern post on which charges for drinks were cut or scored (See page 64.)

65. **scour:** beat (with puns on "score" and on **scour your fault** as "purge away your sin")

66. **maw:** belly (Proverbial: "The belly is the truest clock.")

71. **gave in charge:** i.e., entrusted

74. **how . . . disposed:** i.e., where . . . put

She is so hot because the meat is cold;
The meat is cold because you come not home;
You come not home because you have no stomach;
You have no stomach, having broke your fast. 50
But we that know what 'tis to fast and pray
Are penitent for your default today.

ANTIPHOLUS ⌈OF SYRACUSE⌉
Stop in your wind, sir. Tell me this, I pray:
Where have you left the money that I gave you?

DROMIO OF EPHESUS
O, sixpence that I had o' Wednesday last 55
To pay the saddler for my mistress' crupper?
The saddler had it, sir; I kept it not.

ANTIPHOLUS ⌈OF SYRACUSE⌉
I am not in a sportive humor now.
Tell me, and dally not: where is the money?
We being strangers here, how dar'st thou trust 60
So great a charge from thine own custody?

DROMIO OF EPHESUS
I pray you, jest, sir, as you sit at dinner.
I from my mistress come to you in post;
If I return, I shall be post indeed,
For she will scour your fault upon my pate. 65
Methinks your maw, like mine, should be your
⌈clock,⌉
And strike you home without a messenger.

ANTIPHOLUS ⌈OF SYRACUSE⌉
Come, Dromio, come, these jests are out of season.
Reserve them till a merrier hour than this. 70
Where is the gold I gave in charge to thee?

DROMIO OF EPHESUS
To me, sir? Why, you gave no gold to me!

ANTIPHOLUS ⌈OF SYRACUSE⌉
Come on, sir knave, have done your foolishness,
And tell me how thou hast disposed thy charge.

75. **My charge:** i.e., the order or duty given me

77. **stays for:** i.e., wait for

79. **bestowed:** stowed, placed

80. **sconce:** a slang term for "head"

81. **stands on tricks:** i.e., practices foolery; **undisposed:** unwilling, not inclined (to joke)

86. **pay:** wordplay on **pay** as "beat, flog"

92. **hie you:** hurry

93. **flout:** mock, insult

97. **an:** if

99. **o'erraught:** cheated (past tense of "overreach")

100. **cozenage:** deception, fraud (See longer note to 1.1.0 SD for Ephesus as a city famous for witchcraft and sorcery. Antipholus of Syracuse, in lines 98–105, alludes to its witches and sorcerers, but also constructs Ephesus as being filled with criminals— **jugglers** and **mountebanks**—who defraud through delusion and trickery. See page 24.)

101. **As:** such as; **jugglers:** tricksters, deceivers

DROMIO OF EPHESUS
    My charge was but to fetch you from the mart          75
    Home to your house, the Phoenix, sir, to dinner.
    My mistress and her sister stays for you.
ANTIPHOLUS ⌐OF SYRACUSE⌐
    Now, as I am a Christian, answer me
    In what safe place you have bestowed my money,
    Or I shall break that merry sconce of yours          80
    That stands on tricks when I am undisposed.
    Where is the thousand marks thou hadst of me?
DROMIO OF EPHESUS
    I have some marks of yours upon my pate,
    Some of my mistress' marks upon my shoulders,
    But not a thousand marks between you both.            85
    If I should pay your Worship those again,
    Perchance you will not bear them patiently.
ANTIPHOLUS ⌐OF SYRACUSE⌐
    Thy mistress' marks? What mistress, slave, hast
        thou?
DROMIO OF EPHESUS
    Your Worship's wife, my mistress at the Phoenix,      90
    She that doth fast till you come home to dinner
    And prays that you will hie you home to dinner.
ANTIPHOLUS ⌐OF SYRACUSE, *beating Dromio*⌐
    What, wilt thou flout me thus unto my face,
    Being forbid? There, take you that, sir knave.
DROMIO OF EPHESUS
    What mean you, sir? For God's sake, hold your         95
        hands.
    Nay, an you will not, sir, I'll take my heels.
                              *Dromio* ⌐*of*⌐ *Ephesus exits.*
ANTIPHOLUS ⌐OF SYRACUSE⌐
    Upon my life, by some device or other
    The villain is ⌐o'erraught⌐ of all my money.
    They say this town is full of cozenage,              100
    As nimble jugglers that deceive the eye,

102. **change:** transform
104. **prating mountebanks:** i.e., fast-talking char-
latans
105. **liberties:** i.e., excesses

Notable Difcouery of Coofenage.

*Now daily practifed by fundry lewd per-*
fons , called Connie-catchers, and
Croffe-byters.

Plainely laying open thofe pernitious fleights that hath brought many ignorant men to confufion.

ten for the generall benefit of all Gentlemen, Citizens, Aprentifes, Countrey Farmers
and yeomen, that may hap to fall into the company of fuch coofening companions.

With a delightfull difcourfe of the coofnage of Colliers.

Nafcimur pro patria.       By R. Greene, Maifter of Art

LONDON
Printed by Thomas Scarlet for Thomas Nelfon.
1 5 9 2

"This town is full of cozenage." (1.2.100)
From Robert Greene, *Notable discouery of coosenage . . .* (1592).

Dark-working sorcerers that change the mind,
Soul-killing witches that deform the body,
Disguisèd cheaters, prating mountebanks,
And many suchlike liberties of sin.                    105
If it prove so, I will be gone the sooner.
I'll to the Centaur to go seek this slave.
I greatly fear my money is not safe.

                                        *He exits.*

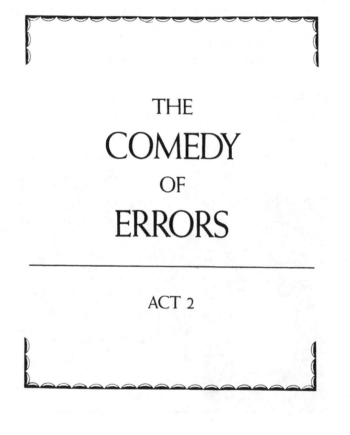

# THE
# COMEDY
## OF
# ERRORS

ACT 2

**2.1** Adriana angrily awaits her husband, who is late for dinner. Dromio (of Ephesus) enters and tells about his meeting with Antipholus (of Syracuse). Adriana, furious that Antipholus has denied that he has a wife, sends Dromio back to fetch him home.

---

8. **Time:** i.e., only time; **see time:** i.e., see the proper moment or opportunity

10. **than ours be more:** i.e., be more than ours

11. **still:** always; **out o' door:** out of the house, away from home

12. **Look when:** whenever; **ill:** badly

A merchant with his goods. (1.1.3)
From Theodor de Bry, *Emblemata . . .* (1593).

# ACT 2

⌈Scene 1⌉

*Enter Adriana, wife to Antipholus ⌈of Ephesus,⌉ with*
*Luciana, her sister.*

ADRIANA
  Neither my husband nor the slave returned
  That in such haste I sent to seek his master?
  Sure, Luciana, it is two o'clock.
LUCIANA
  Perhaps some merchant hath invited him,
  And from the mart he's somewhere gone to dinner.      5
  Good sister, let us dine, and never fret.
  A man is master of his liberty;
  Time is their master, and when they see time
  They'll go or come. If so, be patient, sister.
ADRIANA
  Why should their liberty than ours be more?      10
LUCIANA
  Because their business still lies out o' door.
ADRIANA
  Look when I serve him so, he takes it ⌈ill.⌉
LUCIANA
  O, know he is the bridle of your will.
ADRIANA
  There's none but asses will be bridled so.
LUCIANA
  Why, headstrong liberty is lashed with woe.      15

29

17. **his bound:** i.e., something that confines or limits it

20–25. **Man . . . accords:** See St. Paul's letter to the church in Ephesus, where he writes: "Wives, submit yourselves unto your own husbands, . . . for the husband is the head of the wife" (The Epistle to the Ephesians 5.22–23). The passage also echoes Genesis 1.26, 28, and Psalm 8.4–8. **accords:** concurrence, consent

27. **troubles of the marriage bed:** There may be an echo here of St. Paul's statement that all who marry "shall have trouble in the flesh" (1 Corinthians 7.28).

30. **start some otherwhere:** i.e., pursue some other woman

32. **No marvel . . . pause:** i.e., no wonder she hesitates (to marry)

33. **no other cause:** perhaps, no cause to be otherwise; or, no other ground of action

36. **like weight:** i.e., a comparable burden (Proverbial: "All commend patience, but none can endure to suffer.")

38. **grieve:** oppress, hurt, injure

39. **helpless:** unavailing, useless

40. **like right bereft:** i.e., the same (marriage) rights stolen from you

41. **fool-begged:** foolish; **left:** abandoned

42. **but to try:** if only to test (what you say)

43. **man:** servant

There's nothing situate under heaven's eye
But hath his bound in earth, in sea, in sky.
The beasts, the fishes, and the wingèd fowls
Are their males' subjects and at their controls.
Man, more divine, the master of all these,                    20
Lord of the wide world and wild wat'ry seas,
Endued with intellectual sense and souls,
Of more preeminence than fish and fowls,
Are masters to their females, and their lords.
Then let your will attend on their accords.                   25

ADRIANA
This servitude makes you to keep unwed.

LUCIANA
Not this, but troubles of the marriage bed.

ADRIANA
But, were you wedded, you would bear some sway.

LUCIANA
Ere I learn love, I'll practice to obey.

ADRIANA
How if your husband start some otherwhere?                    30

LUCIANA
Till he come home again, I would forbear.

ADRIANA
Patience unmoved! No marvel though she pause;
They can be meek that have no other cause.
A wretched soul bruised with adversity
We bid be quiet when we hear it cry,                          35
But were we burdened with like weight of pain,
As much or more we should ourselves complain.
So thou, that hast no unkind mate to grieve thee,
With urging helpless patience would relieve me;
But if thou live to see like right bereft,                    40
This fool-begged patience in thee will be left.

LUCIANA
Well, I will marry one day, but to try.
Here comes your man. Now is your husband nigh.

45. **at two hands:** See Dromio's next two speeches (lines 49–50 and 53–55).

49. **told:** (1) spoke; (2) counted out; (3) tolled (This wordplay introduces puns on **understand** (as "grasp the meaning" and "stand under"), **doubtfully** (as "ambiguously" and "dreadfully"), **feel** (as "perceive through the sense of touch" and "be aware of").

50. **Beshrew:** curse (a mild oath)

54. **withal:** at the same time

58. **horn mad:** i.e., mad with rage

60. **cuckold:** A **cuckold** is a man whose wife is unfaithful and who therefore has horns growing out of his forehead. See longer note, pages 165–66.

62. **desired:** asked, requested

A cuckold. (2.1.60)
From *Bagford ballads* (printed in 1878).

*Enter Dromio ⌈of⌉ Ephesus.*

ADRIANA
Say, is your tardy master now at hand?
DROMIO OF EPHESUS  Nay, he's at two hands with me,   45
and that my two ears can witness.
ADRIANA
Say, didst thou speak with him? Know'st thou his
mind?
DROMIO OF EPHESUS
Ay, ay, he told his mind upon mine ear.
Beshrew his hand, I scarce could understand it.   50
LUCIANA  Spake he so doubtfully thou couldst not feel
his meaning?
DROMIO OF EPHESUS  Nay, he struck so plainly I could
too well feel his blows, and withal so doubtfully
that I could scarce understand them.   55
ADRIANA
But say, I prithee, is he coming home?
It seems he hath great care to please his wife.
DROMIO OF EPHESUS
Why, mistress, sure my master is horn mad.
ADRIANA
Horn mad, thou villain?
DROMIO OF EPHESUS         I mean not cuckold mad,   60
But sure he is stark mad.
When I desired him to come home to dinner,
He asked me for a ⌈thousand⌉ marks in gold.
"'Tis dinnertime," quoth I. "My gold," quoth he.
"Your meat doth burn," quoth I. "My gold," quoth   65
he.
"Will you come?" quoth I. "My gold," quoth he.
"Where is the thousand marks I gave thee, villain?"
"The pig," quoth I, "is burned." "My gold," quoth
he.   70

71. **Hang up:** a strong expression of anger or impatience

72. **Out on:** i.e., curses on (an expression of annoyance)

77. **errand:** message; **due unto my tongue:** i.e., which was the duty of my tongue (to deliver)

83. **break thy pate across:** i.e., cut open your head (Dromio responds as if **across** meant "a cross." His words **bless** and **holy** depend on Christian associations with the word **cross,** and play on meanings of **bless** as "wound, hurt, beat" and on **holy** as a pun on "holey, full of holes.")

87. **round:** (1) blunt, plainspoken; (2) spherical

88. **spurn:** literally, kick (See page 62.)

92. **minions:** darlings, favorites (also, hussies); **grace:** favor

94. **homely age:** i.e., age that destroys my beauty

95. **wasted:** (1) squandered; (2) destroyed

96. **discourses, wit:** conversations (**Wit** also means intelligence, understanding, and power of invention.)

97. **voluble:** fluent; **sharp:** keen-witted, sagacious (**Sharp discourse** becomes, in line 98, a knife blunted by **unkindness.**)

"My mistress, sir," quoth I. "Hang up thy mistress!
I know not thy mistress. Out on thy mistress!"
LUCIANA   Quoth who?
DROMIO OF EPHESUS   Quoth my master.
"I know," quoth he, "no house, no wife, no            75
  mistress."
So that my errand, due unto my tongue,
I thank him, I bare home upon my shoulders,
For, in conclusion, he did beat me there.
ADRIANA
Go back again, thou slave, and fetch him home.       80
DROMIO OF EPHESUS
Go back again and be new beaten home?
For God's sake, send some other messenger.
ADRIANA
Back, slave, or I will break thy pate across.
DROMIO OF EPHESUS
And he will bless that cross with other beating.
Between you, I shall have a holy head.               85
ADRIANA
Hence, prating peasant. Fetch thy master home.
DROMIO OF EPHESUS
Am I so round with you as you with me,
That like a football you do spurn me thus?
You spurn me hence, and he will spurn me hither.
If I last in this service, you must case me in leather.  90
                                            ⌜*He exits.*⌝
LUCIANA
Fie, how impatience loureth in your face.
ADRIANA
His company must do his minions grace,
Whilst I at home starve for a merry look.
Hath homely age th' alluring beauty took
From my poor cheek? Then he hath wasted it.          95
Are my discourses dull? Barren my wit?
If voluble and sharp discourse be marred,

99. **gay vestments:** i.e., bright, showy dresses; **affections:** passions; **bait:** tempt, entice
100. **my state:** i.e., the conditions of my life
103. **defeatures:** marred features; **fair:** beauty
105. **pale:** fence or enclosing barrier
106. **from:** i.e., away from; **stale:** i.e., laughingstock, also prostitute
108. **with . . . dispense:** disregard such injuries
109. **otherwhere:** some other place, elsewhere
110. **lets:** hinders
112. **Would . . . detain:** See longer note, page 166. **o' love:** i.e., of his love **detain:** withhold
113. **keep fair quarter with:** maintain good relations with, or conduct toward; **his bed:** i.e., his wife
114. **jewel best enamelèd:** i.e., (even) the best-enameled ornament (See longer note on lines 114–18, page 166.)
115. **his:** i.e., its (Adriana seems to be comparing the jewel to herself or to women in general.)
116. **touch:** possible wordplay on "touching" gold (testing its quality on a touchstone) See page 154.
116–17. **often touching will / Wear gold:** Proverbial: "Gold with often handling is worn to nothing."
117–18. **no man . . . shame:** i.e., no man (i.e., male) with a title or high reputation tarnishes that reputation through his bad behavior
121. **fond:** (1) silly; (2) doting


**2.2** Antipholus (of Syracuse) meets Dromio (of Syracuse), who denies having spoken of Antipholus's wife. Adriana and her sister, Luciana, enter and persuade Antipholus to come to dinner.

Unkindness blunts it more than marble hard.
Do their gay vestments his affections bait?
That's not my fault; he's master of my state.                    100
What ruins are in me that can be found
By him not ruined? Then is he the ground
Of my defeatures. My decayèd fair
A sunny look of his would soon repair.
But, too unruly deer, he breaks the pale                          105
And feeds from home. Poor I am but his stale.

LUCIANA
Self-harming jealousy, fie, beat it hence.

ADRIANA
Unfeeling fools can with such wrongs dispense.
I know his eye doth homage otherwhere,
Or else what lets it but he would be here?                        110
Sister, you know he promised me a chain.
Would that alone o' love he would detain,
So he would keep fair quarter with his bed.
I see the jewel best enamelèd
Will lose his beauty. Yet the gold bides still                    115
That others touch, and often touching will
⌜Wear⌝ gold; ⌜yet⌝ no man that hath a name
By falsehood and corruption doth it shame.
Since that my beauty cannot please his eye,
I'll weep what's left away, and weeping die.                      120

LUCIANA
How many fond fools serve mad jealousy!
                                              ⌜*They*⌝ *exit.*


⌜Scene 2⌝
*Enter Antipholus* ⌜*of Syracuse.*⌝

ANTIPHOLUS ⌜OF SYRACUSE⌝
The gold I gave to Dromio is laid up
Safe at the Centaur, and the heedful slave

4. **computation:** estimation, reckoning
5. **could not speak:** i.e., could not have spoken
7. **humor:** mood
11. **mad:** crazy, insane
17. **the gold's receipt:** i.e., receiving the gold
22. **flout . . . teeth:** i.e., insult me to my face
24. **Hold:** stop, wait a minute; **earnest:** serious (An **earnest** is a small payment to seal a **bargain;** see line 25.)
27. **use you for my fool:** i.e., allow you to jest with me as if your job were to entertain me (like a professional Fool or jester)

Phoenix.
From Conrad Lycosthenes, *Prodigiorum* . . . (1557).

Is wandered forth in care to seek me out.
By computation and mine host's report,
I could not speak with Dromio since at first          5
I sent him from the mart. See, here he comes.

*Enter Dromio ⌜of⌝ Syracuse.*

How now, sir? Is your merry humor altered?
As you love strokes, so jest with me again.
You know no Centaur? You received no gold?
Your mistress sent to have me home to dinner?          10
My house was at the Phoenix? Wast thou mad,
That thus so madly thou didst answer me?

DROMIO OF SYRACUSE
What answer, sir? When spake I such a word?

ANTIPHOLUS ⌜OF SYRACUSE⌝
Even now, even here, not half an hour since.

DROMIO OF SYRACUSE
I did not see you since you sent me hence,              15
Home to the Centaur with the gold you gave me.

ANTIPHOLUS ⌜OF SYRACUSE⌝
Villain, thou didst deny the gold's receipt
And told'st me of a mistress and a dinner,
For which I hope thou felt'st I was displeased.

DROMIO OF SYRACUSE
I am glad to see you in this merry vein.                20
What means this jest, I pray you, master, tell me?

ANTIPHOLUS ⌜OF SYRACUSE⌝
Yea, dost thou jeer and flout me in the teeth?
Think'st thou I jest? Hold, take thou that and that.
                              *Beats Dromio.*

DROMIO OF SYRACUSE
Hold, sir, for God's sake! Now your jest is earnest.
Upon what bargain do you give it me?                   25

ANTIPHOLUS ⌜OF SYRACUSE⌝
Because that I familiarly sometimes
Do use you for my fool and chat with you,

28. **jest upon:** perhaps, amuse yourself with; or, ridicule

29. **make a common of my serious hours:** i.e., treat my serious time frivolously (A **common** is public land.)

30. **make sport:** i.e., amuse themselves

32. **aspect:** face (In astrology, the **aspect** of a planet refers to its position and direction as it looks favorably or unfavorably upon the earth. Accent on the second syllable.)

35. **Sconce:** Dromio plays on this word as a slang term for "head" (as Antipholus means it in line 34); as a "fortification" being subjected to **battering;** and, in line 38, as a "protective screen." (See page 130.)

38. **ensconce:** shelter behind a fortification

39. **seek my wit:** i.e., look for my head **wit:** intelligence

47. **flouting:** mocking (See longer note, page 167.)

48. **urging it:** bringing it forward

50. **out of season:** i.e., at the wrong time

55. **Marry:** a mild oath (originally an oath "by the Virgin Mary")

60–61. **wants that:** lacks that which

Your sauciness will jest upon my love
And make a common of my serious hours.
When the sun shines, let foolish gnats make sport,    30
But creep in crannies when he hides his beams.
If you will jest with me, know my aspect,
And fashion your demeanor to my looks,
Or I will beat this method in your sconce.

DROMIO OF SYRACUSE  "Sconce" call you it? So you    35
would leave battering, I had rather have it a
"head." An you use these blows long, I must get a
sconce for my head and ensconce it too, or else I
shall seek my wit in my shoulders. But I pray, sir,
why am I beaten?    40

ANTIPHOLUS ⌐OF SYRACUSE⌐  Dost thou not know?

DROMIO OF SYRACUSE  Nothing, sir, but that I am
beaten.

ANTIPHOLUS ⌐OF SYRACUSE⌐  Shall I tell you why?

DROMIO OF SYRACUSE  Ay, sir, and wherefore, for they    45
say every why hath a wherefore.

ANTIPHOLUS ⌐OF SYRACUSE⌐  "Why" first: for flouting
me; and then "wherefore": for urging it the second
time to me.

DROMIO OF SYRACUSE
Was there ever any man thus beaten out of season,    50
When in the "why" and the "wherefore" is neither
rhyme nor reason?
Well, sir, I thank you.

ANTIPHOLUS ⌐OF SYRACUSE⌐  Thank me, sir, for what?

DROMIO OF SYRACUSE  Marry, sir, for this something    55
that you gave me for nothing.

ANTIPHOLUS ⌐OF SYRACUSE⌐  I'll make you amends next,
to give you nothing for something. But say, sir, is it
dinnertime?

DROMIO OF SYRACUSE  No, sir, I think the meat wants    60
that I have.

62. **In good time:** An expression of ironical acquiescence which becomes the basis of lengthy wordplay beginning at line 71.

64. **Basting:** To baste is (1) to moisten meat as it roasts; and (2) to beat soundly.

69. **choleric:** Dry meat "engenders choler, planteth anger" *(Taming of the Shrew* 4.1.172).

70. **dry basting:** i.e., dry beating (a harsh beating that does not draw blood)

71–72. **in good time:** i.e., at the appropriate time

72. **There's . . . things:** proverbial

73. **I durst have:** i.e., I would have dared

75. **rule:** maxim, saying

77. **plain bald pate:** Time was usually pictured as bald.

81–82. **fine and recovery:** a legal phrase that describes one method of transferring property

83. **fine:** i.e., fee

84. **lost . . . man:** Human hair was used to make wigs.

86. **excrement:** outgrowth (especially hair or nails)

91. **more hair than wit:** proverbial

92. **Not . . . he:** i.e., every one of whom

92–93. **hath . . . hair:** probably an allusion to the baldness caused by syphilis, an allusion continued in the double entendres of the next several lines of dialogue

95. **plain dealers:** i.e., simple or straightforward men

96–97. **The plainer dealer, the sooner lost:** probably wordplay on "deal" as "to have sexual intercourse" **the sooner lost:** i.e., the sooner he will become infected and lose his hair

ANTIPHOLUS ⌜OF SYRACUSE⌝ In good time, sir, what's
that?

DROMIO OF SYRACUSE Basting.

ANTIPHOLUS ⌜OF SYRACUSE⌝ Well, sir, then 'twill be dry.    65

DROMIO OF SYRACUSE If it be, sir, I pray you eat none of
it.

ANTIPHOLUS ⌜OF SYRACUSE⌝ Your reason?

DROMIO OF SYRACUSE Lest it make you choleric and
purchase me another dry basting.    70

ANTIPHOLUS ⌜OF SYRACUSE⌝ Well, sir, learn to jest in
good time. There's a time for all things.

DROMIO OF SYRACUSE I durst have denied that before
you were so choleric.

ANTIPHOLUS ⌜OF SYRACUSE⌝ By what rule, sir?    75

DROMIO OF SYRACUSE Marry, sir, by a rule as plain as
the plain bald pate of Father Time himself.

ANTIPHOLUS ⌜OF SYRACUSE⌝ Let's hear it.

DROMIO OF SYRACUSE There's no time for a man to
recover his hair that grows bald by nature.    80

ANTIPHOLUS ⌜OF SYRACUSE⌝ May he not do it by fine and
recovery?

DROMIO OF SYRACUSE Yes, to pay a fine for a periwig,
and recover the lost hair of another man.

ANTIPHOLUS ⌜OF SYRACUSE⌝ Why is Time such a niggard    85
of hair, being, as it is, so plentiful an excrement?

DROMIO OF SYRACUSE Because it is a blessing that he
bestows on beasts, and what he hath scanted ⌜men⌝
in hair, he hath given them in wit.

ANTIPHOLUS ⌜OF SYRACUSE⌝ Why, but there's many a    90
man hath more hair than wit.

DROMIO OF SYRACUSE Not a man of those but he hath
the wit to lose his hair.

ANTIPHOLUS ⌜OF SYRACUSE⌝ Why, thou didst conclude
hairy men plain dealers without wit.    95

DROMIO OF SYRACUSE The plainer dealer, the sooner
lost. Yet he loseth it in a kind of jollity.

99. **sound:** valid

100. **sound:** healthy (See note to lines 92–93.)

102–3. **a thing falsing:** i.e., something deceptive

107. **tiring:** i.e., caring for (his) hair; **they:** i.e., hairs

108. **porridge:** soup

118–19. **bald conclusion:** trivial conclusion

119. **soft:** i.e., wait a minute; **wafts:** beckons

120. **look strange:** i.e., act as if we were strangers

121. **aspects:** looks (See note to 2.2.32.)

128–29. **carved to thee:** i.e., **carved** (the **meat**) for you

The three Fates. (1.1.140)
From Vincenzo Cartari, *Imagines deorum* . . . (1581).

ANTIPHOLUS ⌐OF SYRACUSE⌐  For what reason?
DROMIO OF SYRACUSE  For two, and sound ones too.
ANTIPHOLUS ⌐OF SYRACUSE⌐  Nay, not sound, I pray you.  100
DROMIO OF SYRACUSE  Sure ones, then.
ANTIPHOLUS ⌐OF SYRACUSE⌐  Nay, not sure, in a thing
falsing.
DROMIO OF SYRACUSE  Certain ones, then.
ANTIPHOLUS ⌐OF SYRACUSE⌐  Name them.  105
DROMIO OF SYRACUSE  The one, to save the money that
he spends in ⌐tiring;⌐ the other, that at dinner they
should not drop in his porridge.
ANTIPHOLUS ⌐OF SYRACUSE⌐  You would all this time
have proved there is no time for all things.  110
DROMIO OF SYRACUSE  Marry, and did, sir: namely, e'en
no time to recover hair lost by nature.
ANTIPHOLUS ⌐OF SYRACUSE⌐  But your reason was not
substantial why there is no time to recover.
DROMIO OF SYRACUSE  Thus I mend it: Time himself is  115
bald and therefore, to the world's end, will have
bald followers.
ANTIPHOLUS ⌐OF SYRACUSE⌐  I knew 'twould be a bald
conclusion. But soft, who wafts us yonder?

*Enter Adriana, ⌐beckoning them,⌐ and Luciana.*

ADRIANA
  Ay, ay, Antipholus, look strange and frown.  120
  Some other mistress hath thy sweet aspects.
  I am not Adriana, nor thy wife.
  The time was once when thou unurged wouldst vow
  That never words were music to thine ear,
  That never object pleasing in thine eye,  125
  That never touch well welcome to thy hand,
  That never meat sweet-savored in thy taste,
  Unless I spake, or looked, or touched, or carved to
    thee.
  How comes it now, my husband, O, how comes it  130

133. **undividable, incorporate:** i.e., indivisible, united in a legal and physical union (Adriana's view of her marriage)

134. **self's better part:** i.e., soul

135. **tear away thyself:** Adriana at some point takes him by the arm or embraces him.

136–37. **fall . . . gulf:** i.e., let fall a drop of water into the ocean (See note to **lose myself** at 1.2.40.)

141. **dearly:** grievously; **touch . . . quick:** proverbial for "cause you pain"

143,144. **consecrate, contaminate:** i.e., consecrated, contaminated

145. **spurn:** literally, kick

147. **tear . . . brow:** See *Hamlet* 3.4.51–53, where a woman's supposed adultery is said to take "the rose / From the fair forehead of an innocent love" and set "a blister there."

148. **false:** deceitful, treacherous

149. **break it:** perhaps, destroy our marriage; or, perhaps **it** refers to the ring itself

151. **possessed with:** imbued or permeated with; **an adulterate blot:** i.e., the stain of adultery

152. **crime:** sin

155. **strumpeted by thy contagion:** i.e., turned into a strumpet through the contagion of your poisoned flesh

156. **Keep . . . fair league:** i.e., if you keep your covenant or compact

157. **distained:** perhaps, clear of stain (literally, changed in color) See longer note, page 167.

162. **Wants:** lacks; **in all one word:** i.e., in all that you have said

That thou art then estrangèd from thyself?
"Thyself" I call it, being strange to me,
That, undividable, incorporate,
Am better than thy dear self's better part.
Ah, do not tear away thyself from me!          135
For know, my love, as easy mayst thou fall
A drop of water in the breaking gulf,
And take unmingled thence that drop again
Without addition or diminishing,
As take from me thyself and not me too.          140
How dearly would it touch thee to the quick,
Shouldst thou but hear I were licentious
And that this body, consecrate to thee,
By ruffian lust should be contaminate!
Wouldst thou not spit at me, and spurn at me,          145
And hurl the name of husband in my face,
And tear the stained skin off my harlot brow,
And from my false hand cut the wedding ring,
And break it with a deep-divorcing vow?
I know thou canst, and therefore see thou do it.          150
I am possessed with an adulterate blot;
My blood is mingled with the crime of lust;
For if we two be one, and thou play false,
I do digest the poison of thy flesh,
Being strumpeted by thy contagion.          155
Keep then fair league and truce with thy true bed,
I live distained, thou undishonorèd.
ANTIPHOLUS ⌐OF SYRACUSE¬
Plead you to me, fair dame? I know you not.
In Ephesus I am but two hours old,
As strange unto your town as to your talk,          160
Who, every word by all my wit being scanned,
Wants wit in all one word to understand.
LUCIANA
Fie, brother, how the world is changed with you!

164. **use:** treat

172. **course and drift of your compact:** i.e., gist of your plot

178. **by inspiration:** from supernatural sources

179. **ill:** badly; **gravity:** dignity

180. **counterfeit:** practice deceit; **thus grossly:** so obviously

182. **exempt:** taken away, removed

183. **a more:** i.e., still greater

187. **communicate:** partake, share

188. **possess:** i.e., takes possession of: **from:** away from; or, except for

189. **idle:** useless, barren

190. **intrusion:** forced entry

191. **confusion:** ruin

Pruning an arbor. (2.2.190)
From [Thomas Hill,] *The gardeners labyrinth* . . . (1577).

When were you wont to use my sister thus?
She sent for you by Dromio home to dinner.                    165
ANTIPHOLUS ⌐OF SYRACUSE¬  By Dromio?
DROMIO OF SYRACUSE  By me?
ADRIANA
  By thee; and this thou didst return from him:
  That he did buffet thee and, in his blows,
  Denied my house for his, me for his wife.                   170
ANTIPHOLUS ⌐OF SYRACUSE¬
  Did you converse, sir, with this gentlewoman?
  What is the course and drift of your compact?
DROMIO OF SYRACUSE
  I, sir? I never saw her till this time.
ANTIPHOLUS ⌐OF SYRACUSE¬
  Villain, thou liest, for even her very words
  Didst thou deliver to me on the mart.                       175
DROMIO OF SYRACUSE
  I never spake with her in all my life.
ANTIPHOLUS ⌐OF SYRACUSE¬
  How can she thus then call us by our names—
  Unless it be by inspiration?
ADRIANA
  How ill agrees it with your gravity
  To counterfeit thus grossly with your slave,                180
  Abetting him to thwart me in my mood.
  Be it my wrong you are from me exempt,
  But wrong not that wrong with a more contempt.
  Come, I will fasten on this sleeve of thine.
                              ⌐*She takes his arm.*¬
  Thou art an elm, my husband, I a vine,                      185
  Whose weakness, married to thy ⌐stronger¬ state,
  Makes me with thy strength to communicate.
  If aught possess thee from me, it is dross,
  Usurping ivy, brier, or idle moss,
  Who, all for want of pruning, with intrusion                190
  Infect thy sap and live on thy confusion.

192. **moves:** proposes, suggests; **for:** as

196. **know:** understand; **sure uncertainty:** certain or undoubted mystery

197. **entertain:** accept; **offered fallacy:** i.e., this delusion that is being presented to me

198. **spread:** lay the table

199. **beads:** i.e., rosary (See page 80.); **cross me for:** i.e., make the sign of the cross as

200. **the fairy land:** i.e., an enchanted or magic place (For Ephesus as a land of witchcraft and sorcery, see longer note to 1.1.0 SD.)

201. **owls:** often emended to "elves," though **owls** were connected with witchcraft; **sprites:** spirits

203. **suck our breath, pinch:** actions attributed to witches and goblins

206. **sot:** fool

208. **in mind:** i.e., mentally (transformed)

211. **ape:** (1) counterfeit; (2) fool

212. **ass:** dolt, ignoramus

213. **rides:** wordplay on "ride" as "oppress, dominate"; **long for grass:** i.e., long for my freedom (wordplay on the phrase "put out to grass")

ANTIPHOLUS ⌐OF SYRACUSE, *aside*⌐
To me she speaks; she moves me for her theme.
What, was I married to her in my dream?
Or sleep I now and think I hear all this?
What error drives our eyes and ears amiss?          195
Until I know this sure uncertainty
I'll entertain the ⌐offered⌐ fallacy.
LUCIANA
Dromio, go bid the servants spread for dinner.
DROMIO OF SYRACUSE
O, for my beads! I cross me for a sinner.
                              ⌐*He crosses himself.*⌐
This is the fairy land. O spite of spites!          200
We talk with goblins, owls, and sprites.
If we obey them not, this will ensue:
They'll suck our breath, or pinch us black and blue.
LUCIANA
Why prat'st thou to thyself and answer'st not?
Dromio—thou, Dromio—thou snail, thou slug,          205
   thou sot.
DROMIO OF SYRACUSE
I am transformèd, master, am I not?
ANTIPHOLUS ⌐OF SYRACUSE⌐
I think thou art in mind, and so am I.
DROMIO OF SYRACUSE
Nay, master, both in mind and in my shape.
ANTIPHOLUS ⌐OF SYRACUSE⌐
Thou hast thine own form.                           210
DROMIO OF SYRACUSE          No, I am an ape.
LUCIANA
If thou art changed to aught, 'tis to an ass.
DROMIO OF SYRACUSE
'Tis true. She rides me, and I long for grass.
'Tis so. I am an ass; else it could never be
But I should know her as well as she knows me.       215

218. **man:** servant

220. **above:** i.e., upstairs

221. **shrive you of:** i.e., have you confess and give you absolution for

222. **Sirrah:** a term of address to a servant or any (male) social inferior

223. **forth:** away from home

226. **well-advised:** i.e., sane

228. **persever:** persevere (with the accent on the second syllable)

229. **at all adventures:** i.e., whatever the consequences

Title page of an almanac. (1.2.41)
From William Dade, . . . *A new almanacke,
and prognostication* . . . (1636).

ADRIANA
 Come, come, no longer will I be a fool,
 To put the finger in the eye and weep
 Whilst man and master laughs my woes to scorn.
 Come, sir, to dinner.—Dromio, keep the gate.—
 Husband, I'll dine above with you today,                    220
 And shrive you of a thousand idle pranks.
 ⌜*To Dromio.*⌝ Sirrah, if any ask you for your master,
 Say he dines forth, and let no creature enter.—
 Come, sister.—Dromio, play the porter well.
ANTIPHOLUS ⌜OF SYRACUSE, *aside*⌝
 Am I in earth, in heaven, or in hell?                       225
 Sleeping or waking, mad or well-advised?
 Known unto these, and to myself disguised!
 I'll say as they say, and persever so,
 And in this mist at all adventures go.
DROMIO OF SYRACUSE
 Master, shall I be porter at the gate?                      230
ADRIANA
 Ay, and let none enter, lest I break your pate.
LUCIANA
 Come, come, Antipholus, we dine too late.
                                      ⌜*They exit.*⌝

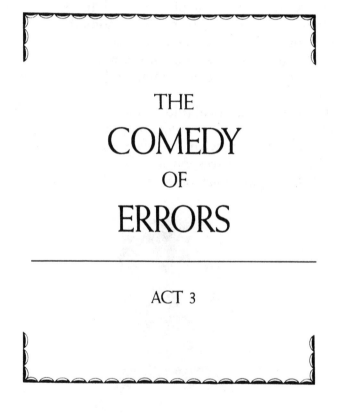

# THE
# COMEDY
## OF
# ERRORS

ACT 3

**3.1**   Antipholus of Ephesus brings a goldsmith and a merchant to his home for dinner. He finds the door locked and, enraged, departs for the Courtesan's house. He sends the goldsmith to fetch a gold chain, which he now decides to give to the Courtesan.

———

1. **excuse us all:** a phrase used to decline an invitation or beg off from doing something (They here enter in midconversation.)
2. **keep not hours:** i.e., am not punctual
4. **carcanet:** an ornamental collar or necklace (See below.)
6. **villain:** i.e., rascal (indicating Dromio); **face me down:** i.e., maintain impudently (that)
8. **charged him with:** i.e., accused him of; or, said he had been made responsible for
12. **hand:** wordplay on **hand** as "handwriting"

A carcanet. (3.1.4)
From Hieronymus Cock, A collection of 16th-century portraits, compiled c. 1555–61 and c. 1577.

# ACT 3

*Enter Antipholus of Ephesus, his man Dromio, Angelo
the goldsmith, and Balthasar the merchant.*

ANTIPHOLUS OF EPHESUS
Good Signior Angelo, you must excuse us all;
My wife is shrewish when I keep not hours.
Say that I lingered with you at your shop
To see the making of her carcanet,
And that tomorrow you will bring it home.          5
But here's a villain that would face me down
He met me on the mart, and that I beat him
And charged him with a thousand marks in gold,
And that I did deny my wife and house.—
Thou drunkard, thou, what didst thou mean by this?   10
DROMIO OF EPHESUS
Say what you will, sir, but I know what I know.
That you beat me at the mart I have your hand to
    show;
If the skin were parchment and the blows you gave
    were ink,                                          15
Your own handwriting would tell you what I think.
ANTIPHOLUS OF EPHESUS
I think thou art an ass.
DROMIO OF EPHESUS          Marry, so it doth appear
By the wrongs I suffer and the blows I bear.

57

20. **at that pass:** i.e., in that predicament

22. **sad:** somber; **cheer:** food, provisions (Proverbial: "Welcome is the best cheer.")

23. **answer:** correspond to, come up to

25. **hold . . . cheap:** i.e., consider . . . of little consequence

26. **dear:** precious

27. **either at:** i.e., whether it serves

28. **scarce:** i.e., scarcely

30. **meat:** food; **common:** commonplace; **churl:** lower-class person or peasant

33–34. **Small cheer . . . feast:** Proverbial: "A cheerful look makes a dish a feast."

36. **cates:** delicacies; **mean:** common, ordinary

36–37. **in good part:** favorably, without offense

40. **soft:** i.e., wait a minute

43. **Mome:** blockhead, fool; **malt-horse:** i.e., stupid slave (literally, a horse on a treadmill that grinds malt in a brewery); **capon:** eunuch (literally, castrated cock); **coxcomb:** fool (literally, the cap worn by a professional Fool); **patch:** dolt, clown (See pages 146, 142, and 60.)

44–45. **sit down at the hatch:** i.e., be quiet (Proverbial: "It is good to have a hatch before the door"— i.e., keep your tongue behind your teeth.) A **hatch** was the lower half of a divided door or gate.

I should kick being kicked and, being at that pass,     20
You would keep from my heels and beware of an ass.
ANTIPHOLUS OF EPHESUS
You're sad, Signior Balthasar. Pray God our cheer
May answer my goodwill and your good welcome
    here.
BALTHASAR
I hold your dainties cheap, sir, and your welcome     25
    dear.
ANTIPHOLUS OF EPHESUS
O Signior Balthasar, either at flesh or fish
A table full of welcome makes scarce one dainty
    dish.
BALTHASAR
Good meat, sir, is common; that every churl affords.     30
ANTIPHOLUS OF EPHESUS
And welcome more common, for that's nothing but
    words.
BALTHASAR
Small cheer and great welcome makes a merry
    feast.
ANTIPHOLUS OF EPHESUS
Ay, to a niggardly host and more sparing guest.     35
But though my cates be mean, take them in good
    part.
Better cheer may you have, but not with better
    heart.     ⌜*He attempts to open the door.*⌝
But soft! My door is locked. ⌜*To Dromio.*⌝ Go, bid     40
    them let us in.
DROMIO OF EPHESUS
Maud, Bridget, Marian, Ciceley, Gillian, Ginn!
DROMIO OF SYRACUSE, ⌜*within*⌝
Mome, malt-horse, capon, coxcomb, idiot, patch!
Either get thee from the door or sit down at the
    hatch.     45

46. **conjure:** summon a spirit by invoking its proper name (Dromio of Syracuse refers to Dromio of Ephesus's calling out the names of several **wenches.**)

47. **such store:** i.e., so many

50. **stays:** waits

53. **on 's:** i.e., in his

55. **I'll tell you when:** perhaps a version of "When, can you tell?"—a colloquial way of saying no to a ridiculous request; **an:** if

61. **owe:** own

62. **for this time:** i.e., for the time being

66. **mickle:** much

69–70. **thy face . . . an ass:** a puzzling line that has not been satisfactorily explained

A "patch." (3.1.43)
From August Casimir Redel, *Apophtegmata symbolica* . . . [n.d.].

Dost thou conjure for wenches, that thou call'st for
  such store
When one is one too many? Go, get thee from the
  door.

DROMIO OF EPHESUS
What patch is made our porter? My master stays in          50
  the street.

DROMIO OF SYRACUSE, ⌜*within*⌝
Let him walk from whence he came, lest he catch
  cold on 's feet.

ANTIPHOLUS OF EPHESUS
Who talks within there? Ho, open the door.

DROMIO OF SYRACUSE, ⌜*within*⌝
Right, sir, I'll tell you when an you'll tell me          55
  wherefore.

ANTIPHOLUS OF EPHESUS
Wherefore? For my dinner. I have not dined today.

DROMIO OF SYRACUSE, ⌜*within*⌝
Nor today here you must not. Come again when you
  may.

ANTIPHOLUS OF EPHESUS
What art thou that keep'st me out from the house I          60
  owe?

DROMIO OF SYRACUSE, ⌜*within*⌝
The porter for this time, sir, and my name is
  Dromio.

DROMIO OF EPHESUS
O villain, thou hast stolen both mine office and my
  name!                                                       65
The one ne'er got me credit, the other mickle
  blame.
If thou hadst been Dromio today in my place,
Thou wouldst have changed thy face for a name, or
  thy name for an ass.                                        70

71. **coil:** fuss, turmoil

77. **Have at you with:** i.e., I'll attack you with; **shall I . . . staff?** proverbial for "shall I make myself at home?"

78. **another:** i.e., another proverb

78–79. **When, can you tell:** See note to line 55, above.

82. **minion:** hussy; **I hope:** There may be a line missing here. As the text stands, the pattern of rhyming lines is broken, and lines 83–84 make little sense.

85–86. **blow for blow:** perhaps they pound on the door (hence Dromio's **Well struck**), giving physical blows in exchange for the verbal blows from Luce

87. **baggage:** strumpet

"Like a football you do spurn me." (2.1.88)
From Henry Peacham, *Minerua Britanna* . . . (1612).

*Enter Luce ⌜above, unseen by Antipholus of Ephesus*
*and his company.⌝*

LUCE
  What a coil is there, Dromio! Who are those at the
    gate?
DROMIO OF EPHESUS
  Let my master in, Luce.
LUCE                      Faith, no, he comes too late,
  And so tell your master.                                    75
DROMIO OF EPHESUS        O Lord, I must laugh.
  Have at you with a proverb: shall I set in my staff?
LUCE
  Have at you with another: that's—When, can you
    tell?
DROMIO OF SYRACUSE, ⌜*within*⌝
  If thy name be called "Luce," Luce, thou hast           80
    answered him well.
ANTIPHOLUS OF EPHESUS, ⌜*to Luce*⌝
  Do you hear, you minion? You'll let us in, I hope?
LUCE
  I thought to have asked you.
DROMIO OF SYRACUSE, ⌜*within*⌝ And you said no.
DROMIO OF EPHESUS
  So, come help. Well struck! There was blow for          85
    blow.
ANTIPHOLUS OF EPHESUS, ⌜*to Luce*⌝
  Thou baggage, let me in.
LUCE                      Can you tell for whose sake?
DROMIO OF EPHESUS
  Master, knock the door hard.
LUCE                      Let him knock till it ache.      90
ANTIPHOLUS OF EPHESUS
  You'll cry for this, minion, if I beat the door down.
                              ⌜*He beats on the door.*⌝

92. **a pair of stocks:** a heavy timber frame with holes for the ankles (**Stocks** were for punishing disturbers of the peace, among others. See page 90.)

94. **keeps:** i.e., makes, keeps up

95–96. **unruly boys:** rowdy fellows, ruffians

98. **knave:** rogue, villain

99. **this knave:** i.e., the person she called **sir knave**

101. **cheer:** food

103. **part:** depart

107. **something in the wind:** i.e., something the matter (Dromio, in line 109, takes the reference to **wind** literally.)

111. **Your cake here:** This phrase is often emended; **here** is sometimes replaced with "there" or is deleted to avoid repetition later in the line.

A tavern's reckoning post. (1.2.64)
From August Casimir Redel, *Apophtegmata symbolica* . . . [n.d.].

LUCE
What needs all that, and a pair of stocks in the
town?

*Enter Adriana, ⌐above, unseen by Antipholus of Ephesus
and his company.⌐*

ADRIANA
Who is that at the door that keeps all this noise?
DROMIO OF SYRACUSE, ⌐*within*⌐
By my troth, your town is troubled with unruly        95
boys.
ANTIPHOLUS OF EPHESUS
Are you there, wife? You might have come before.
ADRIANA
Your wife, sir knave? Go, get you from the door.
                                  ⌐*Adriana and Luce exit.*⌐
DROMIO OF EPHESUS
If you went in pain, master, this knave would go
sore.                                                 100
ANGELO, ⌐*to Antipholus of Ephesus*⌐
Here is neither cheer, sir, nor welcome. We would
fain have either.
BALTHASAR
In debating which was best, we shall part with
neither.
DROMIO OF EPHESUS
They stand at the door, master. Bid them welcome      105
hither.
ANTIPHOLUS OF EPHESUS
There is something in the wind, that we cannot get
in.
DROMIO OF EPHESUS
You would say so, master, if your garments were
thin.                                                 110
Your cake here is warm within; you stand here in
the cold.

113. **mad as a buck:** proverbial
114. **bought and sold:** i.e., betrayed
118. **break a word:** i.e., exchange words
118-19. **words are but wind:** proverbial
120-21. **break it not behind:** wordplay on "to break wind" (i.e., to expel intestinal gas)
122. **thou want'st breaking:** i.e., you're asking to be broken; **Out upon thee:** i.e., curses on you (In the following line, Dromio takes the word **out** literally, and asks to come **in**); **hind:** fellow, boor
125-26. **when fowls . . . fin:** i.e., never
127. **crow:** crowbar
131. **pluck a crow:** proverbial for "settle accounts"
136. **suspect:** suspicion
138. **Once this:** i.e., to sum up, in short

A horse with bridle and crupper. (1.2.56)
From Cesare Fiaschi, *Trattato dell'imbrigliare . . . caualli . . .* (1614).

It would make a man mad as a buck to be so
  bought and sold.

ANTIPHOLUS OF EPHESUS
Go, fetch me something. I'll break ope the gate.          115

DROMIO OF SYRACUSE, ⌜*within*⌝
Break any breaking here, and I'll break your knave's
  pate.

DROMIO OF EPHESUS
A man may break a word with ⌜you,⌝ sir, and words
  are but wind,
Ay, and break it in your face, so he break it not          120
  behind.

DROMIO OF SYRACUSE, ⌜*within*⌝
It seems thou want'st breaking. Out upon thee, hind!

DROMIO OF EPHESUS
Here's too much "Out upon thee!" I pray thee, let
  me in.

DROMIO OF SYRACUSE, ⌜*within*⌝
Ay, when fowls have no feathers and fish have no          125
  fin.

ANTIPHOLUS OF EPHESUS, ⌜*to Dromio of Ephesus*⌝
Well, I'll break in. Go, borrow me a crow.

DROMIO OF EPHESUS
A crow without feather? Master, mean you so?
For a fish without a fin, there's a fowl without a
  feather.—          130
If a crow help us in, sirrah, we'll pluck a crow
  together.

ANTIPHOLUS OF EPHESUS
Go, get thee gone. Fetch me an iron crow.

BALTHASAR
Have patience, sir. O, let it not be so.
Herein you war against your reputation,          135
And draw within the compass of suspect
Th' unviolated honor of your wife.
Once this: your long experience of ⌜her⌝ wisdom,

141. **excuse:** i.e., offer an explanation for
142. **made:** i.e., made fast
147. **offer:** attempt
148. **stirring passage:** i.e., busy traffic
149. **vulgar:** public; **of:** about
150. **And that supposèd:** i.e., and it will be believed; **common rout:** rabble
151. **ungallèd estimation:** uninjured reputation
154. **upon succession:** i.e., by giving birth to new slander
157. **in despite of mirth:** i.e., in spite of mockery
158. **discourse:** conversation
162. **withal:** i.e., with
164. **by this:** i.e., by this time
165. **Porpentine:** i.e., Porcupine

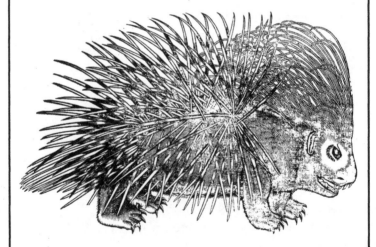

A porcupine. (3.1.165)
From Edward Topsell, *The historie of foure-footed beastes* . . . (1607).

Her sober virtue, years, and modesty
Plead on ⌈her⌉ part some cause to you unknown.          140
And doubt not, sir, but she will well excuse
Why at this time the doors are made against you.
Be ruled by me; depart in patience,
And let us to the Tiger all to dinner,
And about evening come yourself alone          145
To know the reason of this strange restraint.
If by strong hand you offer to break in
Now in the stirring passage of the day,
A vulgar comment will be made of it;
And that supposèd by the common rout          150
Against your yet ungallèd estimation
That may with foul intrusion enter in
And dwell upon your grave when you are dead;
For slander lives upon succession,
Forever housèd where it gets possession.          155

ANTIPHOLUS OF EPHESUS
You have prevailed. I will depart in quiet
And, in despite of mirth, mean to be merry.
I know a wench of excellent discourse,
Pretty and witty, wild and yet, too, gentle.
There will we dine. This woman that I mean,          160
My wife—but, I protest, without desert—
Hath oftentimes upbraided me withal;
To her will we to dinner. ⌈*To Angelo.*⌉ Get you home
And fetch the chain; by this, I know, 'tis made.
Bring it, I pray you, to the Porpentine,          165
For there's the house. That chain will I bestow—
Be it for nothing but to spite my wife—
Upon mine hostess there. Good sir, make haste.
Since mine own doors refuse to entertain me,
I'll knock elsewhere, to see if they'll disdain me.          170

ANGELO
I'll meet you at that place some hour hence.

**3.2** Antipholus (of Syracuse) falls in love with Adriana's sister, Luciana. Dromio (of Syracuse) is claimed by Adriana's kitchen maid as her betrothed. The two Syracusans decide that Luciana and the kitchen maid are witches, and Antipholus sends Dromio to the harbor to book immediate passage. The goldsmith enters and gives Antipholus the chain.

---

2. **office:** duty, responsibility, function
3. **spring:** i.e., springtime; **love-springs:** young springs or shoots of love (See page 132.)
9–10. **Muffle . . . blindness:** i.e., hide your false love by disguising it
13. **fair:** pleasingly, plausibly; **become disloyalty:** perhaps, be attractive in your infidelity
14. **harbinger:** host; forerunner (Proverbial: "Vice is often clothed in virtue's habit.")
15. **fair:** beautiful (Proverbial: "Fair face, foul heart.")
16. **carriage:** bearing; behavior
17. **What . . . acquainted:** i.e., why should she be informed
18. **simple:** foolish; **attaint:** dishonor, disgrace
19. **truant . . . bed:** i.e., be unfaithful **truant with:** wander or stray from
20. **board:** i.e., mealtime (The phrase "bed and board" described a full marriage relationship.)
21. **Shame . . . managèd:** i.e., if properly managed, a shameful life can have a spurious honor
22. **Ill deeds . . . word:** Proverbial: "To do evil and then brag of it is a double wickedness."
24. **Being compact of credit:** i.e., since we are composed of trust

*(continued)*

ANTIPHOLUS OF EPHESUS
Do so. This jest shall cost me some expense.

*They exit.*

┌Scene 2┐
*Enter* ┌*Luciana*┐ *with Antipholus of Syracuse.*

┌LUCIANA┐
And may it be that you have quite forgot
    A husband's office? Shall, Antipholus,
Even in the spring of love thy love-springs rot?
    Shall love, in ┌building,┐ grow so ┌ruinous?┐
If you did wed my sister for her wealth,                    5
    Then for her wealth's sake use her with more
        kindness.
Or if you like elsewhere, do it by stealth—
    Muffle your false love with some show of
        blindness.                                          10
Let not my sister read it in your eye;
    Be not thy tongue thy own shame's orator;
Look sweet, speak fair, become disloyalty;
    Apparel vice like virtue's harbinger.
Bear a fair presence, though your heart be tainted.        15
    Teach sin the carriage of a holy saint.
Be secret-false. What need she be acquainted?
    What simple thief brags of his own ┌attaint?┐
'Tis double wrong to truant with your bed
    And let her read it in thy looks at board.              20
Shame hath a bastard fame, well managèd;
    Ill deeds is doubled with an evil word.
Alas, poor women, make us ┌but┐ believe,
    Being compact of credit, that you love us.
Though others have the arm, show us the sleeve;            25
    We in your motion turn, and you may move us.

26. **We . . . us:** probably a metaphor from Ptolemaic astronomy, in which the **motion** of one celestial body (or of the "first mover" or the crystalline sphere) causes another also to **turn**

29. **'Tis holy sport:** perhaps, it is a pious pastime; **be . . . vain:** perhaps, speak empty words

31. **else:** i.e., other than that

32. **wonder:** i.e., miracle; **hit of:** come upon, light upon

36. **Lay open:** reveal; **gross:** dull, stupid; **conceit:** imagination, thought

38. **folded:** i.e., hidden (literally, enclosed as in a fold)

46. **decline:** incline, lean toward

47. **train:** entice, allure; **mermaid:** i.e., Siren (See page 74 and longer note, page 167.); **note:** song

48. **flood:** (1) sea tide; (2) downpour

49. **Siren:** See longer note to 3.2.47 and page 82.

54. **light:** not heavy, able to float; also, perhaps, wanton

55. **reason so:** talk that way

56. **mated:** astounded, stupefied; also, provided with a mate

Then, gentle brother, get you in again.
    Comfort my sister, cheer her, call her ⌜wife.⌝
'Tis holy sport to be a little vain
    When the sweet breath of flattery conquers strife.        30
ANTIPHOLUS OF SYRACUSE
    Sweet mistress—what your name is else I know not,
    Nor by what wonder you do hit of mine—
Less in your knowledge and your grace you show not
    Than our earth's wonder, more than earth divine.
Teach me, dear creature, how to think and speak.        35
    Lay open to my earthy gross conceit,
Smothered in errors, feeble, shallow, weak,
    The folded meaning of your words' deceit.
Against my soul's pure truth why labor you
    To make it wander in an unknown field?        40
Are you a god? Would you create me new?
    Transform me, then, and to your power I'll yield.
But if that I am I, then well I know
    Your weeping sister is no wife of mine,
Nor to her bed no homage do I owe.        45
    Far more, far more, to you do I decline.
O, train me not, sweet mermaid, with thy note
    To drown me in thy ⌜sister's⌝ flood of tears.
Sing, Siren, for thyself, and I will dote.
    Spread o'er the silver waves thy golden hairs,        50
And as a ⌜bed⌝ I'll take ⌜them⌝ and there lie,
    And in that glorious supposition think
He gains by death that hath such means to die.
    Let love, being light, be drownèd if she sink.
LUCIANA
    What, are you mad that you do reason so?        55
ANTIPHOLUS OF SYRACUSE
    Not mad, but mated—how, I do not know.
LUCIANA
    It is a fault that springeth from your eye.

58. **by:** i.e. nearby

61. **wink:** close one's eyes; **night:** i.e., darkness

68. **aim:** goal

69. **My sole . . . claim:** i.e., my only heaven on this earth and my only claim to heaven (after death)

75. **soft:** i.e., wait a minute

80. **man:** servant

84. **besides myself:** wordplay (here and in lines 85–86) on this phrase as meaning: (1) beside myself, i.e., out of my wits; (2) alongside or in addition to myself

A mermaid. (3.2.47)
From August Casimir Redel, *Apophtegmata symbolica* . . . [n.d.].

ANTIPHOLUS OF SYRACUSE
For gazing on your beams, fair sun, being by.
LUCIANA
Gaze when you should, and that will clear your
  sight.                                                          60
ANTIPHOLUS OF SYRACUSE
As good to wink, sweet love, as look on night.
LUCIANA
Why call you me "love"? Call my sister so.
ANTIPHOLUS OF SYRACUSE
Thy sister's sister.
LUCIANA                 That's my sister.
ANTIPHOLUS OF SYRACUSE                 No,                        65
It is thyself, mine own self's better part,
Mine eye's clear eye, my dear heart's dearer heart,
My food, my fortune, and my sweet hope's aim,
My sole earth's heaven, and my heaven's claim.
LUCIANA
All this my sister is, or else should be.                        70
ANTIPHOLUS OF SYRACUSE
Call thyself "sister," sweet, for I am thee.
Thee will I love, and with thee lead my life;
Thou hast no husband yet, nor I no wife.
Give me thy hand.
LUCIANA               O soft, sir. Hold you still.                75
I'll fetch my sister to get her goodwill.     *She exits.*

         *Enter Dromio* ⌜*of*⌝ *Syracuse,* ⌜*running.*⌝

ANTIPHOLUS OF SYRACUSE  Why, how now, Dromio.
  Where runn'st thou so fast?
DROMIO OF SYRACUSE  Do you know me, sir? Am I
  Dromio? Am I your man? Am I myself?                             80
ANTIPHOLUS OF SYRACUSE  Thou art Dromio, thou art
  my man, thou art thyself.
DROMIO OF SYRACUSE  I am an ass, I am a woman's
  man, and besides myself.

87–88. **am due to:** belong to, am the property of

98. **without:** unless

99. **sir-reverence:** i.e., "saving your reverence" (an apology for being about to mention something indecent or unsavory)

106. **warrant:** guarantee; **rags:** ragged clothes

107. **a Poland winter:** i.e., as long as winter lasts in Poland, known at the time for its severe winters

113. **go overshoes:** i.e., be ankle-deep

116. **in grain:** indelible (**Grain** was a "fast" or permanent dye.) **Noah's flood:** See Genesis 6–8.

119. **Nell:** Traditionally thought to be the same character called Luce in 3.1.71–92.

Noah's flood. (3.2.116)
From Johann Basilius Herold, *Heydenweldt* . . . (1554).

ANTIPHOLUS OF SYRACUSE  What woman's man? And     85
how besides thyself?

DROMIO OF SYRACUSE  Marry, sir, besides myself I am
due to a woman, one that claims me, one that
haunts me, one that will have me.

ANTIPHOLUS OF SYRACUSE  What claim lays she to thee?     90

DROMIO OF SYRACUSE  Marry, sir, such claim as you
would lay to your horse, and she would have me as
a beast; not that I being a beast she would have me,
but that she, being a very beastly creature, lays
claim to me.     95

ANTIPHOLUS OF SYRACUSE  What is she?

DROMIO OF SYRACUSE  A very reverend body, ay, such a
one as a man may not speak of without he say
"sir-reverence." I have but lean luck in the match,
and yet is she a wondrous fat marriage.     100

ANTIPHOLUS OF SYRACUSE  How dost thou mean a "fat
marriage"?

DROMIO OF SYRACUSE  Marry, sir, she's the kitchen
wench, and all grease, and I know not what use to
put her to but to make a lamp of her and run from     105
her by her own light. I warrant her rags and the
tallow in them will burn a Poland winter. If she lives
till doomsday, she'll burn a week longer than the
whole world.

ANTIPHOLUS OF SYRACUSE  What complexion is she of?     110

DROMIO OF SYRACUSE  Swart like my shoe, but her face
nothing like so clean kept. For why? She sweats. A
man may go overshoes in the grime of it.

ANTIPHOLUS OF SYRACUSE  That's a fault that water will
mend.     115

DROMIO OF SYRACUSE  No, sir, 'tis in grain; Noah's flood
could not do it.

ANTIPHOLUS OF SYRACUSE  What's her name?

DROMIO OF SYRACUSE  Nell, sir, but her name ⌐and⌐

120. **an ell:** (1) 45 inches; (2) a Nell

130. **bogs:** soft marshy land (John Speed writes, in 1614, of certain places of Ireland "which of their softness are usually termed bogs.") The word also had a coarse meaning somehow related to a privy or to excretion.

135–36. **armed and reverted . . . heir:** This passage seems an allusion to contemporary civil wars in France that involved Henri of Navarre, the **heir** of Henri III, and to the "French disease" or venereal disease, which caused the forehead to be **armed** with eruptions and the hair to recede or "revert."

138. **chalky cliffs:** (1) chalk cliffs of Dover; (2) her teeth

140. **salt rheum:** (1) mucus; (2) English Channel (which lies between England and France and is overlooked by the Dover cliffs)

148. **declining:** bending down; **aspect:** See note to 2.2.32.

149. **armadas of carracks:** fleets of large ships or galleons (See page 92.)

150. **ballast:** i.e., ballasted, loaded

151–52. **Belgia, the Netherlands:** parts of the region known as the Low Countries

154. **diviner:** magician, sorcerer

three quarters—that's an ell and three quarters— 120
will not measure her from hip to hip.

ANTIPHOLUS OF SYRACUSE Then she bears some
breadth?

DROMIO OF SYRACUSE No longer from head to foot than
from hip to hip. She is spherical, like a globe. I 125
could find out countries in her.

ANTIPHOLUS OF SYRACUSE In what part of her body
stands Ireland?

DROMIO OF SYRACUSE Marry, sir, in her buttocks. I
found it out by the bogs. 130

ANTIPHOLUS OF SYRACUSE Where Scotland?

DROMIO OF SYRACUSE I found it by the barrenness,
hard in the palm of the hand.

ANTIPHOLUS OF SYRACUSE Where France?

DROMIO OF SYRACUSE In her forehead, armed and 135
reverted, making war against her heir.

ANTIPHOLUS OF SYRACUSE Where England?

DROMIO OF SYRACUSE I looked for the chalky cliffs, but
I could find no whiteness in them. But I guess it
stood in her chin, by the salt rheum that ran 140
between France and it.

ANTIPHOLUS OF SYRACUSE Where Spain?

DROMIO OF SYRACUSE Faith, I saw it not, but I felt it hot
in her breath.

ANTIPHOLUS OF SYRACUSE Where America, the Indies? 145

DROMIO OF SYRACUSE O, sir, upon her nose, all o'er-
embellished with rubies, carbuncles, sapphires,
declining their rich aspect to the hot breath of
Spain, who sent whole armadas of carracks to be
ballast at her nose. 150

ANTIPHOLUS OF SYRACUSE Where stood Belgia, the
Netherlands?

DROMIO OF SYRACUSE O, sir, I did not look so low. To
conclude: this drudge or diviner laid claim to me,

155. **assured:** betrothed
156. **privy:** (1) secret, private; (2) personal
156–57. **mark of:** i.e., birthmark on
158. **amazed:** astounded, stupefied
162. **curtal dog:** i.e., a bobtailed dog
163. **turn i' th' wheel:** i.e., turn the roasting spit
164. **hie thee presently:** i.e., go immediately; **Post:** i.e., go quickly, as if by post-horse; **road:** harbor
165. **An if:** i.e., if
167. **bark:** ship; **put forth:** sets out, embarks
170. **pack:** hurry off
173. **inhabit:** reside, dwell
177. **Possessed with:** endowed with, possessing
178. **enchanting:** (1) delightful; (2) spellbinding (i.e., able to put one under a spell)
180. **guilty to:** i.e., guilty of
181. **stop:** close up, as with a stopper or plug (See longer note to **mermaid,** 3.2.47.)

A rosary. (2.2.199)
From Cesare Vecellio, *Habiti antichi et moderni* . . . (1598).

called me Dromio, swore I was assured to her, told     155
me what privy marks I had about me, as the mark
of my shoulder, the mole in my neck, the great wart
on my left arm, that I, amazed, ran from her as a
witch.
And, I think, if my breast had not been made of     160
    faith, and my heart of steel,
She had transformed me to a curtal dog and made
    me turn i' th' wheel.

ANTIPHOLUS OF SYRACUSE
Go, hie thee presently. Post to the road.
An if the wind blow any way from shore,     165
I will not harbor in this town tonight.
If any bark put forth, come to the mart,
Where I will walk till thou return to me.
If everyone knows us, and we know none,
'Tis time, I think, to trudge, pack, and be gone.     170

DROMIO OF SYRACUSE
As from a bear a man would run for life,
So fly I from her that would be my wife.     *He exits.*

ANTIPHOLUS OF SYRACUSE
There's none but witches do inhabit here,
And therefore 'tis high time that I were hence.
She that doth call me husband, even my soul     175
Doth for a wife abhor. But her fair sister,
Possessed with such a gentle sovereign grace,
Of such enchanting presence and discourse,
Hath almost made me traitor to myself.
But lest myself be guilty to self wrong,     180
I'll stop mine ears against the mermaid's song.

*Enter Angelo with the chain.*

ANGELO
Master Antipholus.

ANTIPHOLUS OF SYRACUSE     Ay, that's my name.

185. **ta'en:** i.e., overtaken, caught

186. **The chain unfinished:** i.e., the fact that the chain was not finished

188. **What . . . yourself:** i.e., whatever pleases you

189. **I . . . not:** i.e., I did not place an order for it

191. **withal:** with it

198. **vain:** foolish, devoid of sense or wisdom

199. **so fair an offered chain:** perhaps, a chain so courteously offered; or, perhaps, the offer of such a beautiful chain

200. **shifts:** tricks, fraud

202. **stay:** wait

203. **straight:** immediately

Sirens. (3.2.47–49, 181)
From Geoffrey Whitney, *A choice of emblemes . . .* (1586).

ANGELO
I know it well, sir. Lo, here's the chain.
I thought to have ta'en you at the Porpentine;        185
The chain unfinished made me stay thus long.
⌐*He gives Antipholus a chain.*¬
ANTIPHOLUS OF SYRACUSE
What is your will that I shall do with this?
ANGELO
What please yourself, sir. I have made it for you.
ANTIPHOLUS OF SYRACUSE
Made it for me, sir? I bespoke it not.
ANGELO
Not once, nor twice, but twenty times you have.        190
Go home with it, and please your wife withal,
And soon at supper time I'll visit you
And then receive my money for the chain.
ANTIPHOLUS OF SYRACUSE
I pray you, sir, receive the money now,
For fear you ne'er see chain nor money more.        195
ANGELO
You are a merry man, sir. Fare you well.        *He exits.*
ANTIPHOLUS OF SYRACUSE
What I should think of this I cannot tell,
But this I think: there's no man is so vain
That would refuse so fair an offered chain.
I see a man here needs not live by shifts        200
When in the streets he meets such golden gifts.
I'll to the mart, and there for Dromio stay.
If any ship put out, then straight away.
                                        *He exits.*

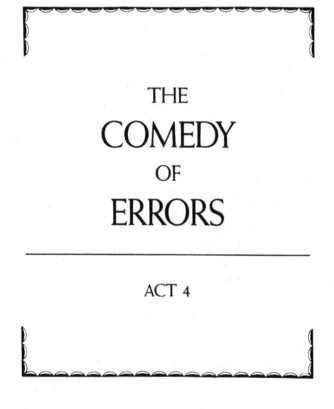

# THE
# COMEDY
## OF
# ERRORS

ACT 4

**4.1** Antipholus (of Ephesus) sends Dromio (of Ephesus) to buy a rope's end to beat Adriana. The goldsmith demands the money Antipholus owes him for the chain. Antipholus denies having received the chain and refuses to pay. The goldsmith has Antipholus arrested. Dromio (of Syracuse) enters with news of a ship on which he has booked passage. Antipholus (of Ephesus) sends Dromio (of Syracuse) to Adriana for money for bail.

———

1. **Pentecost:** i.e., the seventh Sunday after Easter, on which the Christian church celebrates the descent of the Holy Spirit on the Apostles
2. **since:** i.e., since that time
3. **I had not:** I would not have (i.e., **importuned you**)
4. **want guilders:** i.e., need (or lack) money
5. **present:** immediate; **satisfaction:** i.e., payment
6. **attach:** arrest
7. **Even just:** i.e., exactly
8. **growing to me by:** i.e., coming due or accruing to me from
9. **in the instant:** i.e., at the very moment
10. **of me:** i.e., from me
11. **the same:** i.e., the chain
12. **Pleaseth you:** i.e., if you please to (a polite phrase)
13. **discharge my bond:** i.e., pay my debt
14. **That labor:** i.e., the labor of walking to his house

# ACT 4

―――――――――――

## Scene 1

*Enter a ⌐Second⌐ Merchant, ⌐Angelo the⌐ Goldsmith, and an Officer.*

⌐SECOND⌐ MERCHANT, ⌐to Angelo⌐
You know since Pentecost the sum is due,
And since I have not much importuned you,
Nor now I had not, but that I am bound
To Persia and want guilders for my voyage.
Therefore make present satisfaction, 5
Or I'll attach you by this officer.

ANGELO
Even just the sum that I do owe to you
Is growing to me by Antipholus.
And in the instant that I met with you,
He had of me a chain. At five o'clock 10
I shall receive the money for the same.
Pleaseth you walk with me down to his house,
I will discharge my bond and thank you too.

*Enter Antipholus ⌐of⌐ Ephesus ⌐and⌐ Dromio ⌐of Ephesus⌐ from the Courtesan's.*

OFFICER
That labor may you save. See where he comes.

ANTIPHOLUS OF EPHESUS, ⌐to Dromio of Ephesus⌐
While I go to the goldsmith's house, go thou 15

87

16. **rope's end:** piece of rope used for flogging; **bestow:** employ, apply (with an ironic sense also of "give as a present")

21. **I . . . rope:** Dromio's indignant exit line has not been satisfactorily explained.

22. **holp up:** i.e., helped, benefited

25. **Belike:** perhaps

27. **Saving:** with all respect to; **humor:** mood

29. **chargeful fashion:** expensive or costly craftsmanship

30. **three-odd ducats:** i.e., three ducats plus a bit more (See longer note to 1.1.8.)

31. **stand debted:** i.e., am in debt

32. **presently discharged:** immediately paid

33. **stays but for it:** i.e., waits only for the money

34. **present money:** ready money, money at hand

36. **the stranger:** i.e., the Second Merchant

38. **on the receipt thereof:** i.e., on receiving the chain

41. **time enough:** i.e., soon enough

42. **about you:** i.e., somewhere on your person

And buy a rope's end. That will I bestow
Among my wife and ⌜her⌝ confederates
For locking me out of my doors by day.
But soft. I see the goldsmith. Get thee gone.
Buy thou a rope, and bring it home to me.                    20
DROMIO ⌜OF EPHESUS⌝
 I buy a thousand pound a year! I buy a rope!
                                                    *Dromio exits.*
ANTIPHOLUS OF EPHESUS, ⌜*to Angelo*⌝
 A man is well holp up that trusts to you!
 I promisèd your presence and the chain,
 But neither chain nor goldsmith came to me.
 Belike you thought our love would last too long   25
 If it were chained together, and therefore came not.
ANGELO, ⌜*handing a paper to Antipholus of Ephesus*⌝
 Saving your merry humor, here's the note
 How much your chain weighs to the utmost carat,
 The fineness of the gold, and chargeful fashion,
 Which doth amount to three-odd ducats more     30
 Than I stand debted to this gentleman.
 I pray you, see him presently discharged,
 For he is bound to sea, and stays but for it.
ANTIPHOLUS OF EPHESUS
 I am not furnished with the present money.
 Besides, I have some business in the town.      35
 Good signior, take the stranger to my house,
 And with you take the chain, and bid my wife
 Disburse the sum on the receipt thereof.
 Perchance I will be there as soon as you.
ANGELO
 Then you will bring the chain to her yourself.   40
ANTIPHOLUS OF EPHESUS
 No, bear it with you lest I come not time enough.
ANGELO
 Well, sir, I will. Have you the chain about you?

43. **An if:** i.e., if

46. **wind and tide:** Proverbial: "Time and tide stay for no man."

47. **to blame:** blameworthy, at fault

48. **dalliance:** talk, conversation

50. **chid:** scolded

52. **dispatch:** make haste

55. **even now:** just now

56. **send by me some token:** i.e., send some token along with me

57. **run this humor out of breath:** i.e., take this joke too far

59. **brook this dalliance:** tolerate this waste of time

60. **whe'er:** i.e., whether; **answer:** i.e., pay

61. **him:** i.e., Angelo

". . . a pair of stocks." (3.1.92)

From [T]homas [F]ella, *A book of diverse devices* (1585–1622).

ANTIPHOLUS OF EPHESUS
  An if I have not, sir, I hope you have,
  Or else you may return without your money.
ANGELO
  Nay, come, I pray you, sir, give me the chain. 45
  Both wind and tide stays for this gentleman,
  And I, to blame, have held him here too long.
ANTIPHOLUS OF EPHESUS
  Good Lord! You use this dalliance to excuse
  Your breach of promise to the Porpentine.
  I should have chid you for not bringing it, 50
  But, like a shrew, you first begin to brawl.
⌜SECOND⌝ MERCHANT, ⌜*to Angelo*⌝
  The hour steals on. I pray you, sir, dispatch.
ANGELO, ⌜*to Antipholus of Ephesus*⌝
  You hear how he importunes me. The chain!
ANTIPHOLUS OF EPHESUS
  Why, give it to my wife, and fetch your money.
ANGELO
  Come, come. You know I gave it you even now. 55
  Either send the chain, or send ⌜by me⌝ some token.
ANTIPHOLUS OF EPHESUS
  Fie, now you run this humor out of breath.
  Come, where's the chain? I pray you, let me see it.
⌜SECOND⌝ MERCHANT
  My business cannot brook this dalliance.
  Good sir, say whe'er you'll answer me or no. 60
  If not, I'll leave him to the Officer.
ANTIPHOLUS OF EPHESUS
  I answer you? What should I answer you?
ANGELO
  The money that you owe me for the chain.
ANTIPHOLUS OF EPHESUS
  I owe you none till I receive the chain.
ANGELO
  You know I gave it you half an hour since. 65

68. **stands upon:** affects, involves; **credit:** standing, repute

75. **that I never had:** i.e., for that which I never received

79. **apparently:** obviously, openly

82. **sirrah:** a term of address to a male inferior; **buy this sport:** pay for this game or entertainment

83. **dear:** expensively

84. **metal:** i.e., gold; **answer:** pay for

SPAANSSE CARAKEN

Spanish carracks. (3.2.149)
From Cornelis van Yk, *De Nederlandsche scheeps-bouw-konst open gestelt . . .* (1697).

ANTIPHOLUS OF EPHESUS
You gave me none. You wrong me much to say so.

ANGELO
You wrong me more, sir, in denying it.
Consider how it stands upon my credit.

⌈SECOND⌉ MERCHANT
Well, officer, arrest him at my suit.

OFFICER, ⌈*to Angelo*⌉
I do, and charge you in the Duke's name to obey        70
me.

ANGELO, ⌈*to Antipholus of Ephesus*⌉
This touches me in reputation.
Either consent to pay this sum for me,
Or I attach you by this officer.

ANTIPHOLUS OF EPHESUS
Consent to pay thee that I never had?—        75
Arrest me, foolish fellow, if thou dar'st.

ANGELO, ⌈*to Officer*⌉
Here is thy fee. Arrest him, officer.   ⌈*Giving money.*⌉
I would not spare my brother in this case
If he should scorn me so apparently.

OFFICER, ⌈*to Antipholus of Ephesus*⌉
I do arrest you, sir. You hear the suit.        80

ANTIPHOLUS OF EPHESUS
I do obey thee till I give thee bail.
⌈*To Angelo.*⌉ But, sirrah, you shall buy this sport as
dear
As all the metal in your shop will answer.

ANGELO
Sir, sir, I shall have law in Ephesus,        85
To your notorious shame, I doubt it not.

*Enter Dromio ⌈of⌉ Syracuse from the bay.*

DROMIO OF SYRACUSE
Master, there's a bark of Epidamium
That stays but till her owner comes aboard,

89. **sir . . . sir:** Some editors cut the first **sir** to eliminate its repetition. **bears away:** sails away, leaves; **fraughtage:** freight, cargo

91. **balsamum:** balm; **aqua vitae:** strong drink, usually brandy

92. **in her trim:** fully rigged

94. **master:** either addressed to Antipholus (the equivalent of "sir") or a reference to the ship's "master" or captain

95. **peevish:** silly, senseless

97. **hire waftage:** i.e., book passage **waftage:** conveyance by ship

100. **a rope's end:** i.e., a flogging; or, a halter

103. **list me:** i.e., listen to me

104. **hie thee straight:** hurry immediately

109. **that:** i.e., the **purse of ducats**

112. **Dowsabel:** from *douce et belle,* a general name for a sweetheart (here used ironically to refer to the kitchen wench Nell—or Luce, as she is called earlier)

113. **compass:** (1) attain; (2) encircle, reach around

114. **Thither:** i.e., go there

115. **minds:** intentions, purposes

And then, sir, she bears away. Our fraughtage, sir,
I have conveyed aboard, and I have bought              90
The oil, the balsamum, and aqua vitae.
The ship is in her trim; the merry wind
Blows fair from land. They stay for naught at all
But for their owner, master, and yourself.

ANTIPHOLUS OF EPHESUS
How now? A madman? Why, thou peevish sheep,       95
What ship of Epidamium stays for me?

DROMIO OF SYRACUSE
A ship you sent me to, to hire waftage.

ANTIPHOLUS OF EPHESUS
Thou drunken slave, I sent thee for a rope
And told thee to what purpose and what end.

DROMIO OF SYRACUSE
You sent me for a rope's end as soon.              100
You sent me to the bay, sir, for a bark.

ANTIPHOLUS OF EPHESUS
I will debate this matter at more leisure
And teach your ears to list me with more heed.
To Adriana, villain, hie thee straight.
                              ⌜*He gives a key.*⌝
Give her this key, and tell her in the desk        105
That's covered o'er with Turkish tapestry
There is a purse of ducats. Let her send it.
Tell her I am arrested in the street,
And that shall bail me. Hie thee, slave. Begone.—
On, officer, to prison till it come.               110
                    ⌜*All but Dromio of Syracuse*⌝ *exit.*

DROMIO OF SYRACUSE
To Adriana. That is where we dined,
Where Dowsabel did claim me for her husband.
She is too big, I hope, for me to compass.
Thither I must, although against my will,
For servants must their masters' minds fulfill.    115
                                        *He exits.*

**4.2** Dromio (of Syracuse) tells Adriana about the arrest of Antipholus (of Ephesus). She gives him the money for Antipholus's bail.

---

2. **austerely:** i.e., in an austere manner (It is unclear whether this word is being applied to Luciana or to Antipholus.)

4. **or . . . or:** i.e., either . . . or

6. **heart's meteors tilting:** i.e., conflicting emotions battling **meteors:** i.e., celestial disturbances **tilting:** engaging in formal combat

7. **no right:** i.e., any right

8. **none:** i.e., no right; **spite:** vexation

10. **And true . . . were:** This line is variously explained as a reference by Adriana to Antipholus's strange or distant behavior or to his threatened estrangement from her.

15. **honest suit:** honorable courtship; **move:** persuade, stir the emotions

17. **speak him fair:** i.e., respond civilly or encouragingly to him

19. **hold me still:** i.e., remain silent

20. **his:** i.e., its

21. **He:** Antipholus

22. **shapeless:** unshapely, misshapen

⌜Scene 2⌝
*Enter Adriana and Luciana.*

ADRIANA
Ah, Luciana, did he tempt thee so?
Might'st thou perceive austerely in his eye
That he did plead in earnest, yea or no?
Looked he or red or pale, or sad or merrily?
What observation mad'st thou in this case          5
⌜Of⌝ his heart's meteors tilting in his face?
LUCIANA
First he denied you had in him no right.
ADRIANA
He meant he did me none; the more my spite.
LUCIANA
Then swore he that he was a stranger here.
ADRIANA
And true he swore, though yet forsworn he were.          10
LUCIANA
Then pleaded I for you.
ADRIANA                                    And what said he?
LUCIANA
That love I begged for you he begged of me.
ADRIANA
With what persuasion did he tempt thy love?
LUCIANA
With words that in an honest suit might move.          15
First he did praise my beauty, then my speech.
ADRIANA
Did'st speak him fair?
LUCIANA                                    Have patience, I beseech.
ADRIANA
I cannot, nor I will not hold me still.
My tongue, though not my heart, shall have his will.          20
He is deformèd, crooked, old, and sere,
Ill-faced, worse-bodied, shapeless everywhere,

23. **ungentle:** dishonorable; inhumane

24. **Stigmatical in making:** deformed in build

28. **would herein:** wish that in this case

29. **Far . . . away:** The **lapwing** protects her young by flying away from the nest. Proverbial: "The lapwing cries most when farthest from her nest."

37. **Tartar limbo:** i.e., prison (See longer note, page 167.)

38. **A devil in an everlasting garment:** Dromio's exaggerated account of the arresting officer includes descriptions of the officer's clothes (**buttoned up with steel, all in buff**), his behavior (**pitiless and rough**), and his function (**carries poor souls to hell**). **everlasting garment:** probably the leather uniform of police officers (line 41), though some editors believe that **everlasting** is the name of a fabric.

40. **fairy:** evil spirit (See longer note, page 168.)

41. **buff:** i.e., buff leather (used to make jackets for law officers)

42. **backfriend:** (1) false friend; (2) one who makes an arrest by clapping one on the back; thus **a shoulder clapper**

43–44. **countermands/The passages of:** prohibits people passing through

44. **creeks:** winding paths; **narrow lands:** This phrase has not been satisfactorily explained.

45. **runs counter:** runs in a direction opposite to that of the game being hunted, with wordplay on **counter** as "debtors' prison"; **draws dryfoot:** follows the game merely by the scent of its foot (See page 110.)

48. **hell:** i.e., prison

Vicious, ungentle, foolish, blunt, unkind,
Stigmatical in making, worse in mind.

LUCIANA
Who would be jealous, then, of such a one?                25
No evil lost is wailed when it is gone.

ADRIANA
Ah, but I think him better than I say,
And yet would herein others' eyes were worse.
Far from her nest the lapwing cries away.
My heart prays for him, though my tongue do          30
curse.

*Enter Dromio ⌐of⌐ Syracuse ⌐with the key.⌐*

DROMIO OF SYRACUSE
Here, go—the desk, the purse! Sweet, now make
haste.

LUCIANA
How hast thou lost thy breath?

DROMIO OF SYRACUSE                        By running fast.       35

ADRIANA
Where is thy master, Dromio? Is he well?

DROMIO OF SYRACUSE
No, he's in Tartar limbo, worse than hell.
A devil in an everlasting garment hath him,
One whose hard heart is buttoned up with steel;
A fiend, a fairy, pitiless and rough;                          40
A wolf, nay, worse, a fellow all in buff;
A backfriend, a shoulder clapper, one that
countermands
The passages of alleys, creeks, and narrow lands;
A hound that runs counter and yet draws dryfoot       45
well,
One that before the judgment carries poor souls to
hell.

ADRIANA  Why, man, what is the matter?

50. **I do . . . case:** This line contains a set of puns on **matter** (as [1] legal allegation, [2] substance) and on **case** (as [1] clothing, [2] form or outer container, as opposed to substance).

53. **is in:** i.e., he is in

55. **redemption:** i.e., the money that will redeem him from the **hell** (line 48) of prison

59. **band:** bond (taken by Dromio in line 60 to mean a strip of fabric)

64–65. **strikes one:** Since the words *on* and *one* were almost interchangeable in sound and spelling, Dromio may here be saying "strikes on," but is heard by Adriana to be saying "strikes one."

66. **come back:** i.e., go in reverse

67. **hour:** Some editors have heard puns here on "whore" and "ower." **sergeant:** police officer

69. **fondly:** foolishly

71. **a very bankrout:** a veritable bankrupt

71–72. **owes . . . to season:** This much-debated phrase may be read as playing on the near-equivalency of the words *time* and *season,* so that time itself becomes a bankrupt to the passage of time.

74. **time . . . day:** proverbial

DROMIO OF SYRACUSE

I do not know the matter. He is 'rested on the case.        50

ADRIANA

What, is he arrested? Tell me at whose suit.

DROMIO OF SYRACUSE

I know not at whose suit he is arrested well,
But is in a suit of buff which 'rested him; that can I
tell.
Will you send him, mistress, redemption—the        55
money in his desk?

ADRIANA

Go fetch it, sister. (*Luciana exits.*) This I wonder at,
⌐That⌐ he, unknown to me, should be in debt.
Tell me, was he arrested on a band?

DROMIO OF SYRACUSE

Not on a band, but on a stronger thing:        60
A chain, a chain. Do you not hear it ring?

ADRIANA   What, the chain?

DROMIO OF SYRACUSE

No, no, the bell. 'Tis time that I were gone.
It was two ere I left him, and now the clock strikes
one.        65

ADRIANA

The hours come back. That did I never hear.

DROMIO OF SYRACUSE

O yes, if any hour meet a sergeant, he turns back
for very fear.

ADRIANA

As if time were in debt. How fondly dost thou
reason!        70

DROMIO OF SYRACUSE

Time is a very bankrout and owes more than he's
worth to season.
Nay, he's a thief too. Have you not heard men say
That time comes stealing on by night and day?

75. **he:** i.e., time; **and theft:** i.e., and is also a thief; **a sergeant in:** i.e., a sergeant stands in

77. **Hath he . . . day:** a reference back to lines 67–68

78. **straight:** straightway, at once

80. **conceit:** imagination; also, understanding

**4.3**  Dromio (of Syracuse) gives Antipholus (of Syracuse) the money sent by Adriana. The Courtesan enters and demands the chain that Antipholus is wearing. When he flees, calling her a devil, she decides to tell Adriana that Antipholus is insane.

1. **salute:** greet

4. **tender:** offer

5. **Some other:** i.e., others

9. **therewithal:** in addition

10. **imaginary wiles:** tricks of the imagination

11. **Lapland:** a region legendary at the time for its witches and magicians (See page 114.); **inhabit:** live, dwell

13–14. **got the picture . . . new-appareled:** perhaps, got rid of the officer (who arrested you) See longer note, page 168.

If ⌈he⌉ be in debt and theft, and a sergeant in the        75
    way,
Hath he not reason to turn back an hour in a day?
                *Enter Luciana, ⌈with the purse.⌉*

ADRIANA
Go, Dromio. There's the money. Bear it straight,
And bring thy master home immediately.
                                *⌈Dromio exits.⌉*
Come, sister, I am pressed down with conceit:        80
Conceit, my comfort and my injury.
                                *⌈They⌉ exit.*


                        *⌈Scene 3⌉*
*Enter Antipholus ⌈of⌉ Syracuse, ⌈wearing the chain.⌉*

ANTIPHOLUS OF SYRACUSE
There's not a man I meet but doth salute me
As if I were their well-acquainted friend,
And everyone doth call me by my name.
Some tender money to me; some invite me;
Some other give me thanks for kindnesses;        5
Some offer me commodities to buy.
Even now a tailor called me in his shop
And showed me silks that he had bought for me,
And therewithal took measure of my body.
Sure these are but imaginary wiles,        10
And Lapland sorcerers inhabit here.

            *Enter Dromio ⌈of⌉ Syracuse ⌈with the purse.⌉*

DROMIO OF SYRACUSE   Master, here's the gold you sent
    me for. What, have you got the picture of old Adam
    new-appareled?
ANTIPHOLUS OF SYRACUSE
What gold is this? What Adam dost thou mean?        15

18–19. **calf's . . . Prodigal:** See longer note to 4.3.13–14.

24–25. **gives them a sob and 'rests them:** i.e., allows them a respite and (1) lets them rest, (2) arrests them **sob:** the breathing space allowed a winded horse

26. **decayed:** ruined (financially and/or physically); **durance:** (1) durable, imitation-leather cloth; (2) imprisonment, confinement

27. **sets up his rest:** firmly decides (a term meaning "stakes his all" from the game of primero), with a pun on **rest** as "arrest"

28. **mace:** sergeant's staff; **morris-pike:** weapon supposedly of Moorish origin

31. **of the band:** of the troops

32. **answer it:** i.e., answer for it

33. **band:** bond

34. **rest:** another pun on *rest/arrest*

39. **bark** *Expedition:* i.e., ship named "haste"

41. **hoy:** a small boat designed for fast sailing; **angels:** money (See longer note to 1.1.8.)

42. **deliver you:** i.e., set you free

43. **distract:** distracted, insane

DROMIO OF SYRACUSE  Not that Adam that kept the
Paradise, but that Adam that keeps the prison; he
that goes in the calf's skin that was killed for the
Prodigal; he that came behind you, sir, like an evil
angel, and bid you forsake your liberty.                    20

ANTIPHOLUS OF SYRACUSE  I understand thee not.

DROMIO OF SYRACUSE  No? Why, 'tis a plain case: he
that went like a bass viol in a case of leather; the
man, sir, that, when gentlemen are tired, gives
them a sob and 'rests them; he, sir, that takes pity    25
on decayed men and gives them suits of durance; he
that sets up his rest to do more exploits with his
mace than a morris-pike.

ANTIPHOLUS OF SYRACUSE  What, thou mean'st an
officer?                                                    30

DROMIO OF SYRACUSE  Ay, sir, the sergeant of the band;
he that brings any man to answer it that breaks his
band; one that thinks a man always going to bed
and says "God give you good rest."

ANTIPHOLUS OF SYRACUSE  Well, sir, there rest in your   35
foolery. Is there any ships puts forth tonight? May
we be gone?

DROMIO OF SYRACUSE  Why, sir, I brought you word an
hour since that the bark *Expedition* put forth tonight, and then were you hindered by the sergeant       40
to tarry for the hoy *Delay*. Here are the angels that
you sent for to deliver you.      ⌜*He gives the purse.*⌝

ANTIPHOLUS OF SYRACUSE
The fellow is distract, and so am I,
And here we wander in illusions.
Some blessèd power deliver us from hence!                45

*Enter a Courtesan.*

COURTESAN
Well met, well met, Master Antipholus.

49. **avoid:** depart

53. **devil's dam:** The **devil's dam** (i.e., mother) was proverbially more evil than the devil. **habit:** clothing

54. **light wench:** immoral woman; **thereof comes:** i.e., for that reason it happens

55. **damn:** a pun on *damn/dam*

56–57. **they appear . . . light:** probably a reference to 2 Corinthians 11.14, "Satan himself is transformed into an angel of light."

58. **ergo:** therefore; **burn:** perhaps, cause venereal disease

61. **mend:** complete; supplement

62–63. **spoon meat:** soft or liquid food

63. **bespeak:** arrange for, order

65–66. **he must . . . devil:** proverbial

68. **sorceress:** See note to 1.2.100.

69. **conjure:** charge, order (**Conjure** also carries here its meanings of [1] to bring out or convey away by magic incantation, and [2] to exorcise an evil spirit.)

71. **for my diamond:** i.e., in exchange for my ring

73–75. **parings . . . cherrystone:** small items used by witches in casting spells

76. **An if:** i.e., if

77. **the devil . . . chain:** perhaps a reference to Revelation 20.1–2: "And I saw an angel come down from heaven, having . . . a great chain in his hand. And he took . . . the devil . . . , and he bound him a thousand years."

I see, sir, you have found the goldsmith now.
Is that the chain you promised me today?

ANTIPHOLUS OF SYRACUSE
Satan, avoid! I charge thee, tempt me not.

DROMIO OF SYRACUSE
Master, is this Mistress Satan?                          50

ANTIPHOLUS OF SYRACUSE          It is the devil.

DROMIO OF SYRACUSE  Nay, she is worse; she is the
devil's dam, and here she comes in the habit of a
light wench. And thereof comes that the wenches
say "God damn me"; that's as much to say "God     55
make me a light wench." It is written they appear
to men like angels of light. Light is an effect of fire,
and fire will burn: ergo, light wenches will burn.
Come not near her.

COURTESAN
Your man and you are marvelous merry, sir.          60
Will you go with me? We'll mend our dinner here.

DROMIO OF SYRACUSE  Master, if ⌜you⌝ do, expect spoon
meat, or bespeak a long spoon.

ANTIPHOLUS OF SYRACUSE  Why, Dromio?

DROMIO OF SYRACUSE  Marry, he must have a long     65
spoon that must eat with the devil.

ANTIPHOLUS OF SYRACUSE, ⌜to the Courtesan⌝
Avoid then, fiend! What tell'st thou me of supping?
Thou art, as you are all, a sorceress.
I conjure thee to leave me and be gone.

COURTESAN
Give me the ring of mine you had at dinner          70
Or, for my diamond, the chain you promised,
And I'll be gone, sir, and not trouble you.

DROMIO OF SYRACUSE  Some devils ask but the parings
of one's nail, a rush, a hair, a drop of blood, a pin, a
nut, a cherrystone; but she, more covetous, would     75
have a chain. Master, be wise. An if you give it her,
the devil will shake her chain and fright us with it.

80. **Avaunt:** begone

81. **"Fly pride," says the peacock:** Dromio perhaps suggests that for this devil to ask Antipholus not to cheat her is like the peacock, proudest of birds, warning others to beware of pride. Proverbial: "Proud as a peacock." (See page 124.)

83. **out of doubt:** i.e., there is no doubt that

84. **Else would he:** i.e., otherwise he would; **demean himself:** behave himself

85. **ducats:** gold coins

92. **Belike:** perhaps; probably

94. **hie home:** hurry directly

96. **perforce:** forcibly

**4.4** Antipholus (of Ephesus), under arrest, beats Dromio (of Ephesus) for bringing a rope's end instead of the money for bail. Adriana, Luciana, and the Courtesan enter with Dr. Pinch, who has been employed to cure Antipholus's reported insanity. Officers bind Antipholus and Dromio (of Ephesus), and Dr. Pinch has them carried off. Antipholus and Dromio (of Syracuse) enter with their swords drawn, frightening Adriana and the others, who think the madmen have escaped from Dr. Pinch.

---

1. **Fear me not:** i.e., don't doubt or distrust me
2. **so much:** i.e., as much
3. **To warrant thee:** i.e., as security
4. **wayward:** perverse, refractory

COURTESAN
  I pray you, sir, my ring or else the chain.
  I hope you do not mean to cheat me so.
ANTIPHOLUS OF SYRACUSE
  Avaunt, thou witch!—Come, Dromio, let us go.       80
DROMIO OF SYRACUSE   "Fly pride," says the peacock.
  Mistress, that you know.
                    ⌐Antipholus and Dromio⌐ exit.
COURTESAN
  Now, out of doubt Antipholus is mad;
  Else would he never so demean himself.
  A ring he hath of mine worth forty ducats,       85
  And for the same he promised me a chain.
  Both one and other he denies me now.
  The reason that I gather he is mad,
  Besides this present instance of his rage,
  Is a mad tale he told today at dinner       90
  Of his own doors being shut against his entrance.
  Belike his wife, acquainted with his fits,
  On purpose shut the doors against his way.
  My way is now to hie home to his house
  And tell his wife that, being lunatic,       95
  He rushed into my house and took perforce
  My ring away. This course I fittest choose,
  For forty ducats is too much to lose.
                              ⌐She exits.⌐


                    ⌐Scene 4⌐
*Enter Antipholus ⌐of⌐ Ephesus with a Jailer, ⌐the Officer.⌐*

ANTIPHOLUS OF EPHESUS
  Fear me not, man. I will not break away.
  I'll give thee, ere I leave thee, so much money,
  To warrant thee, as I am 'rested for.
  My wife is in a wayward mood today

5. **lightly:** easily, readily

6. **I should be attached:** i.e., I have been arrested

7 SD. **rope's end:** See note to 4.1.16.

11. **warrant you:** i.e., promise; **pay:** beat, flog

15. **serve you . . . rate:** perhaps, provide you with five hundred at that price

16. **To what end:** i.e., for what purpose

17–18. **to that end:** i.e., for that purpose

21–22. **'tis for me . . . adversity:** proverbial: "patience in adversity"

23. **Good now:** a phrase introducing a command or request

26. **senseless:** without human sense

28. **senseless:** incapable of sensing

30. **sensible in:** i.e., able to feel, intelligent about

"A hound that . . . draws dryfoot." (4.2.45)
From [George Turberville,] *The noble art of venerie . . .* (1611).

And will not lightly trust the messenger    5
That I should be attached in Ephesus.
I tell you, 'twill sound harshly in her ears.

*Enter Dromio* ⌜*of*⌝ *Ephesus with a rope's end.*

Here comes my man. I think he brings the
    money.
How now, sir? Have you that I sent you for?    10
DROMIO OF EPHESUS, ⌜*handing over the rope's end*⌝
    Here's that, I warrant you, will pay them all.
ANTIPHOLUS OF EPHESUS    But where's the money?
DROMIO OF EPHESUS
    Why, sir, I gave the money for the rope.
ANTIPHOLUS OF EPHESUS
    Five hundred ducats, villain, for a rope?
DROMIO OF EPHESUS
    I'll serve you, sir, five hundred at the rate.    15
ANTIPHOLUS OF EPHESUS
    To what end did I bid thee hie thee home?
DROMIO OF EPHESUS    To a rope's end, sir, and to that
    end am I returned.
ANTIPHOLUS OF EPHESUS, ⌜*beating Dromio*⌝
    And to that end, sir, I will welcome you.
OFFICER    Good sir, be patient.    20
DROMIO OF EPHESUS    Nay, 'tis for me to be patient. I am
    in adversity.
OFFICER    Good now, hold thy tongue.
DROMIO OF EPHESUS    Nay, rather persuade him to hold
    his hands.    25
ANTIPHOLUS OF EPHESUS    Thou whoreson, senseless
    villain.
DROMIO OF EPHESUS    I would I were senseless, sir, that
    I might not feel your blows.
ANTIPHOLUS OF EPHESUS    Thou art sensible in nothing    30
    but blows, and so is an ass.

32. **I am an ass, indeed:** See longer note to 2.2.47 for echoes of the Balaam's ass story.

33. **long ears:** Proverbial: "An ass is known by his long ears." There may also be wordplay on *ears/years*, with Dromio saying that he has been an ass for serving Antipholus for so long.

35. **at his hands:** from him (with a pun on the literal meaning of **hands**)

39. **from home:** i.e., away

41. **wont:** i.e., is accustomed to doing with

45. **respice finem:** Proverbial: "Consider your end"—i.e., your death. Perhaps **your end** also puns on "your buttocks," the target of the "rope's end" (with the familiar pun on *respice funem*, "consider the rope").

46. **like the parrot:** Parrots were taught to repeat "rope" as a comic threat of death on the gallows.

48. **still:** continually

51. **Doctor:** a title given to a teacher or a learned man; **conjurer:** As a schoolmaster, Pinch would know and teach Latin; thus he would be thought to be able to conjure spirits and exorcise demons.

52. **true sense:** i.e., right mind

53. **please you what:** i.e., pay you whatever pleases you

54. **sharp:** irritable

55. **Mark:** notice; **ecstasy:** frenzy, madness

DROMIO OF EPHESUS  I am an ass, indeed; you may
prove it by my long ears.—I have served him from
the hour of my nativity to this instant, and have
nothing at his hands for my service but blows.          35
When I am cold, he heats me with beating; when I
am warm, he cools me with beating. I am waked
with it when I sleep, raised with it when I sit,
driven out of doors with it when I go from home,
welcomed home with it when I return. Nay, I bear it     40
on my shoulders as a beggar wont her brat, and I
think when he hath lamed me, I shall beg with it
from door to door.

*Enter Adriana, Luciana, Courtesan, and a Schoolmaster*
*called Pinch.*

ANTIPHOLUS OF EPHESUS
Come, go along. My wife is coming yonder.
DROMIO OF EPHESUS  Mistress, *respice finem*, respect     45
your end, or rather, the prophecy like the parrot,
"Beware the rope's end."
ANTIPHOLUS OF EPHESUS  Wilt thou still talk?
                                              *Beats Dromio.*
COURTESAN, ⌜*to Adriana*⌝
How say you now? Is not your husband mad?
ADRIANA
His incivility confirms no less.—                        50
Good Doctor Pinch, you are a conjurer;
Establish him in his true sense again,
And I will please you what you will demand.
LUCIANA
Alas, how fiery and how sharp he looks!
COURTESAN
Mark how he trembles in his ecstasy.                     55
PINCH, ⌜*to Antipholus of Ephesus*⌝
Give me your hand, and let me feel your pulse.

58. **I charge thee, Satan:** One explanation of insanity was possession by the devil.

60. **hie thee straight:** i.e., go at once

62. **doting:** foolish, crazy

64. **minion:** hussy

65. **this companion:** i.e., Doctor Pinch (**Companion** is often used as a term of contempt.); **saffron:** saffron yellow, an orange-yellow color

68. **denied:** forbidden

70. **would you:** i.e., I wish you

71. **slanders:** disgraces; or, disgraceful actions

76. **Perdie:** *par Dieu,* French for "by God"

78. **Sans fable:** i.e., without falsehood

A Lapland witch practicing her art. (4.3.11)
From Olaus Magnus, *Historia de gentibus septentrionalibus . . .* (1555).

ANTIPHOLUS OF EPHESUS, ⌐*striking Pinch*⌐
There is my hand, and let it feel your ear.
PINCH
I charge thee, Satan, housed within this man,
To yield possession to my holy prayers,
And to thy state of darkness hie thee straight.          60
I conjure thee by all the saints in heaven.
ANTIPHOLUS OF EPHESUS
Peace, doting wizard, peace. I am not mad.
ADRIANA
O, that thou wert not, poor distressèd soul!
ANTIPHOLUS OF EPHESUS
You minion, you, are these your customers?
Did this companion with the saffron face          65
Revel and feast it at my house today
Whilst upon me the guilty doors were shut
And I denied to enter in my house?
ADRIANA
O husband, God doth know you dined at home,
Where would you had remained until this time,          70
Free from these slanders and this open shame.
ANTIPHOLUS OF EPHESUS
"Dined at home"? ⌐*To Dromio.*⌐ Thou villain, what
sayest thou?
DROMIO OF EPHESUS
Sir, sooth to say, you did not dine at home.
ANTIPHOLUS OF EPHESUS
Were not my doors locked up and I shut out?          75
DROMIO OF EPHESUS
Perdie, your doors were locked, and you shut out.
ANTIPHOLUS OF EPHESUS
And did not she herself revile me there?
DROMIO OF EPHESUS
Sans fable, she herself reviled you there.
ANTIPHOLUS OF EPHESUS
Did not her kitchen maid rail, taunt, and scorn me?

80. **Certes:** certainly; **vestal:** i.e., virgin (Vestal virgins were the priestesses of Vesta in ancient Rome. See below. The word is used here ironically.)

84. **soothe:** humor, encourage; **contraries:** perhaps, statements that deny the obvious truth

85. **The fellow:** i.e., Dromio; **finds his vein:** i.e., understands his disposition

86. **yielding to:** i.e., going along with; **humors:** indulges; **frenzy:** madness

87. **suborned:** secretly bribed

91. **a rag of money:** i.e., a farthing

97. **possessed:** See note to 4.4.58.

98. **deadly:** deathlike

99. **They must . . . room:** This was a standard treatment for insanity.

100. **forth:** i.e., out

A vestal virgin. (4.4.80)
From Johann Basilius Herold, *Heydenweldt* . . . (1554).

DROMIO OF EPHESUS
  Certes, she did; the kitchen vestal scorned you.     80
ANTIPHOLUS OF EPHESUS
  And did not I in rage depart from thence?
DROMIO OF EPHESUS
  In verity you did.—My bones bears witness,
  That since have felt the vigor of his rage.
ADRIANA, ⌐to Pinch¬
  Is 't good to soothe him in these contraries?
PINCH
  It is no shame. The fellow finds his vein     85
  And, yielding to him, humors well his frenzy.
ANTIPHOLUS OF EPHESUS, ⌐to Adriana¬
  Thou hast suborned the goldsmith to arrest me.
ADRIANA
  Alas, I sent you money to redeem you
  By Dromio here, who came in haste for it.
DROMIO OF EPHESUS
  Money by me? Heart and goodwill you might,     90
  But surely, master, not a rag of money.
ANTIPHOLUS OF EPHESUS
  Went'st not thou to her for a purse of ducats?
ADRIANA
  He came to me, and I delivered it.
LUCIANA
  And I am witness with her that she did.
DROMIO OF EPHESUS
  God and the rope-maker bear me witness     95
  That I was sent for nothing but a rope.
PINCH
  Mistress, both man and master is possessed.
  I know it by their pale and deadly looks.
  They must be bound and laid in some dark room.
ANTIPHOLUS OF EPHESUS, ⌐to Adriana¬
  Say wherefore didst thou lock me forth today.     100

106. **Dissembling:** lying

108. **pack:** gang

109. **abject scorn:** despicable object of mockery

111. **sport:** game or entertainment

112 SD. **offer:** attempt

113. **More company:** i.e., more men come to hold him

116. **suffer:** allow

117. **make a rescue:** a legal phrase meaning to remove a person forcibly from legal custody

120. **frantic:** insane

121. **peevish:** foolish; malicious

123. **outrage:** grievous injury; **displeasure:** wrong, offense

A courtesan. (4.3.45 SD)
From Johann Theodor de Bry, *Proscenium vitae humanae, siue emblematum secularium* . . . (1627).

⌐*To Dromio of Ephesus.*⌐ And why dost thou deny the
  bag of gold?

ADRIANA
  I did not, gentle husband, lock thee forth.

DROMIO OF EPHESUS
  And, gentle master, I received no gold.
  But I confess, sir, that we were locked out.          105

ADRIANA
  Dissembling villain, thou speak'st false in both.

ANTIPHOLUS OF EPHESUS
  Dissembling harlot, thou art false in all,
  And art confederate with a damnèd pack
  To make a loathsome abject scorn of me.
  But with these nails I'll pluck out these false eyes     110
  That would behold in me this shameful sport.

ADRIANA
  O bind him, bind him! Let him not come near me.

  *Enter three or four, and offer to bind him. He strives.*

PINCH
  More company! The fiend is strong within him.

LUCIANA
  Ay me, poor man, how pale and wan he looks!

ANTIPHOLUS OF EPHESUS
  What, will you murder me?—Thou jailer, thou,            115
  I am thy prisoner. Wilt thou suffer them
  To make a rescue?

OFFICER                Masters, let him go.
  He is my prisoner, and you shall not have him.

PINCH
  Go, bind this man, for he is frantic too.               120
                          ⌐*Dromio is bound.*⌐

ADRIANA, ⌐*to Officer*⌐
  What wilt thou do, thou peevish officer?
  Hast thou delight to see a wretched man
  Do outrage and displeasure to himself?

125. **required of:** demanded from

126. **discharge:** recompense

128. **knowing how the debt grows:** i.e., once I know how the debt accrued

130. **unhappy:** wretched, ill-fated

132. **am . . . bond for you:** (1) am tied up here because of you; (2) have signed a document promising to pay (a certain amount of money) for you

133. **Out on thee:** i.e., curse you; **mad:** i.e., madden, enrage

136. **Cry "The devil!":** i.e., (1) refuse to cooperate ("The devil!" was an expression of impatience or strong negation.); (2) show how mad you are by calling on the devil

137. **idly:** incoherently, deliriously

Doomsday. (3.2.108)
From Thomas Fisher, *A Series of Antient . . . Paintings . . . on the Walls of the Chapel . . . at Stratford upon Avon* (1804).

OFFICER
He is my prisoner. If I let him go,
The debt he owes will be required of me.          125
ADRIANA
I will discharge thee ere I go from thee.
Bear me forthwith unto his creditor,
And knowing how the debt grows, I will pay it.—
Good Master Doctor, see him safe conveyed
Home to my house. O most unhappy day!          130
ANTIPHOLUS OF EPHESUS   O most unhappy strumpet!
DROMIO OF EPHESUS
Master, I am here entered in bond for you.
ANTIPHOLUS OF EPHESUS
Out on thee, villain! Wherefore dost thou mad me?
DROMIO OF EPHESUS
Will you be bound for nothing? Be mad, good
    master.                                          135
Cry "The devil!"
LUCIANA
God help poor souls! How idly do they talk!
ADRIANA, ⌐to Pinch⌐
Go bear him hence.
            ⌐*Pinch and his men*⌐ *exit* ⌐*with Antipholus*
                        *and Dromio of Ephesus.*⌐
        *Officer, Adriana, Luciana, Courtesan remain.*
                    Sister, go you with me.
⌐*To Officer.*⌐ Say now whose suit is he arrested at.          140
OFFICER
One Angelo, a goldsmith. Do you know him?
ADRIANA
I know the man. What is the sum he owes?
OFFICER
Two hundred ducats.
ADRIANA                    Say, how grows it due?
OFFICER
Due for a chain your husband had of him.          145

147. **Whenas:** i.e., when

150. **Straight after:** i.e., immediately afterward

153. **at large:** i.e., in detail

155. **naked:** unsheathed

158. **witches:** See note to 1.2.100.

159. **would be your wife:** i.e., claimed to be your wife

163–64. **speak us fair:** i.e., speak courteously to us

164. **Methinks:** it seems to me; **gentle:** courteous, generous

167. **still:** always

A centaur.
From Dirck Pietersz Pers, *Bellerophon* . . . [n.d.].

ADRIANA
He did bespeak a chain for me but had it not.

COURTESAN
Whenas your husband all in rage today
Came to my house and took away my ring,
The ring I saw upon his finger now,
Straight after did I meet him with a chain.                    150

ADRIANA
It may be so, but I did never see it.—
Come, jailer, bring me where the goldsmith is.
I long to know the truth hereof at large.

*Enter Antipholus ⌈of⌉ Syracuse with his rapier drawn,*
*and Dromio ⌈of⌉ Syracuse.*

LUCIANA
God for Thy mercy, they are loose again!

ADRIANA
And come with naked swords. Let's call more help    155
To have them bound again.

OFFICER                          Away! They'll kill us.
         *Run all out as fast as may be, frighted.*
   ⌈*Antipholus and Dromio of Syracuse remain.*⌉

ANTIPHOLUS OF SYRACUSE
I see these witches are afraid of swords.

DROMIO OF SYRACUSE
She that would be your wife now ran from you.

ANTIPHOLUS OF SYRACUSE
Come to the Centaur. Fetch our stuff from thence.    160
I long that we were safe and sound aboard.

DROMIO OF SYRACUSE    Faith, stay here this night. They
will surely do us no harm. You saw they speak us
fair, give us gold. Methinks they are such a gentle
nation that, but for the mountain of mad flesh that    165
claims marriage of me, I could find in my heart to
stay here still, and turn witch.

"'Fly pride,' says the peacock." (4.3.81)
From Johann Theodor de Bry, *Proscenium vitae humanae, siue emblematum secularium . . .* (1627).

ANTIPHOLUS OF SYRACUSE
  I will not stay tonight for all the town.
  Therefore, away, to get our stuff aboard.

                                    *They exit.*

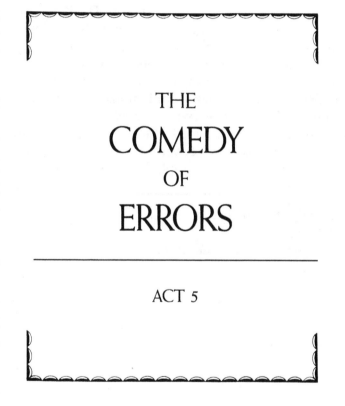

# THE
# COMEDY
## OF
# ERRORS

## ACT 5

**5.1** Adriana finds Antipholus (of Syracuse) with his sword drawn and orders that he and Dromio be bound. The Syracusans escape into a nearby priory. The Abbess of the priory refuses to make them come out. The Duke enters, bringing Egeon to execution. Adriana begs the Duke to remove Antipholus from the priory. When Antipholus and Dromio (of Ephesus) enter, having escaped from Dr. Pinch, the Duke listens to conflicting accounts of what Antipholus and Dromio have done. Egeon says that Antipholus is his son, but Antipholus denies knowing him. The Abbess enters with Antipholus and Dromio (of Syracuse). The day's confusions are explained when the two sets of twins are seen side by side. Antipholus (of Syracuse) declares again his love for Luciana. The Abbess recognizes Egeon as her lost husband and the twin Antipholuses as her lost sons.

---

8. **might bear:** i.e., is worth
10. **self:** same
11. **forswore:** denied on oath

# *ACT 5*

---

*Enter the ⌜Second⌝ Merchant and ⌜Angelo⌝ the*
*Goldsmith.*

**ANGELO**
I am sorry, sir, that I have hindered you,
But I protest he had the chain of me,
Though most dishonestly he doth deny it.
⌜**SECOND**⌝ **MERCHANT**
How is the man esteemed here in the city?
**ANGELO**
Of very reverend reputation, sir,                              5
Of credit infinite, highly beloved,
Second to none that lives here in the city.
His word might bear my wealth at any time.
⌜**SECOND**⌝ **MERCHANT**
Speak softly. Yonder, as I think, he walks.

*Enter Antipholus and Dromio ⌜of Syracuse⌝ again,*
*⌜Antipholus wearing the chain.⌝*

**ANGELO**
'Tis so, and that self chain about his neck                   10
Which he forswore most monstrously to have.
Good sir, draw near to me. I'll speak to him.—
Signior Antipholus, I wonder much
That you would put me to this shame and trouble,
And not without some scandal to yourself,                     15

129

16. **circumstance:** detailed argument
18. **charge:** expense, trouble
19. **honest:** honorable
20. **but for staying on:** i.e., except for being delayed by
28. **resort:** i.e., visit, live
29. **impeach:** attack, discredit
31. **presently:** at once; **stand:** i.e., defend yourself
32 SD. **draw:** i.e., draw their swords
33. **Hold:** i.e., stop, wait
34. **within him:** inside his guard
37. **spoiled:** destroyed, seriously injured

Battering a wall. (2.2.35–36)
From Guillaume Du Choul, *Los discursos de la religion* . . . (1579).

With circumstance and oaths so to deny
This chain, which now you wear so openly.
Besides the charge, the shame, imprisonment,
You have done wrong to this my honest friend,
Who, but for staying on our controversy,                    20
Had hoisted sail and put to sea today.
This chain you had of me. Can you deny it?

ANTIPHOLUS ⌜OF SYRACUSE⌝
I think I had. I never did deny it.

⌜SECOND⌝ MERCHANT
Yes, that you did, sir, and forswore it too.

ANTIPHOLUS ⌜OF SYRACUSE⌝
Who heard me to deny it or forswear it?                      25

⌜SECOND⌝ MERCHANT
These ears of mine, thou know'st, did hear thee.
Fie on thee, wretch. 'Tis pity that thou liv'st
To walk where any honest men resort.

ANTIPHOLUS ⌜OF SYRACUSE⌝
Thou art a villain to impeach me thus.
I'll prove mine honor and mine honesty                      30
Against thee presently if thou dar'st stand.

⌜SECOND⌝ MERCHANT
I dare, and do defy thee for a villain.     *They draw.*

*Enter Adriana, Luciana, Courtesan, and others.*

ADRIANA
Hold, hurt him not, for God's sake. He is mad.—
Some get within him; take his sword away.
Bind Dromio too, and bear them to my house!                 35

DROMIO OF SYRACUSE
Run, master, run. For God's sake, take a house.
This is some priory. In, or we are spoiled.
                    ⌜*Antipholus and Dromio of Syracuse*⌝
                              *exit to the Priory.*

*Enter Lady Abbess.*

39. **distracted:** insane
44. **possession:** See note to 4.4.58.
45. **heavy:** gloomy; **sour:** sullen, morose
48. **Ne'er brake:** i.e., never broke; **rage:** madness
49. **wrack of sea:** i.e., shipwreck
51. **Strayed his affection:** i.e., caused his affection to stray
55. **except:** unless
61. **Haply:** perhaps

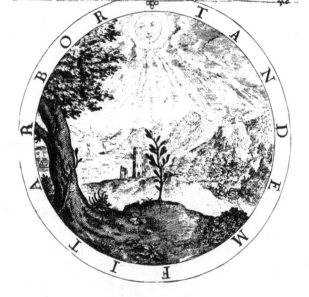

*Though very* ſmall, *at* firſt, *it be,*
*A* Sprout, *at length, becomes a* Tree.

A young spring or shoot. (3.2.3)
From George Wither, *A collection of emblemes* . . . (1635).

ABBESS
    Be quiet, people. Wherefore throng you hither?
ADRIANA
    To fetch my poor distracted husband hence.
    Let us come in, that we may bind him fast          40
    And bear him home for his recovery.
ANGELO
    I knew he was not in his perfect wits.
⌜SECOND⌝ MERCHANT
    I am sorry now that I did draw on him.
ABBESS
    How long hath this possession held the man?
ADRIANA
    This week he hath been heavy, sour, sad,          45
    And much different from the man he was.
    But till this afternoon his passion
    Ne'er brake into extremity of rage.
ABBESS
    Hath he not lost much wealth by wrack of sea?
    Buried some dear friend? Hath not else his eye          50
    Strayed his affection in unlawful love,
    A sin prevailing much in youthful men
    Who give their eyes the liberty of gazing?
    Which of these sorrows is he subject to?
ADRIANA
    To none of these, except it be the last,          55
    Namely, some love that drew him oft from home.
ABBESS
    You should for that have reprehended him.
ADRIANA
    Why, so I did.
ABBESS          Ay, but not rough enough.
ADRIANA
    As roughly as my modesty would let me.          60
ABBESS
    Haply in private.

62. **assemblies:** social gatherings
64. **copy:** theme, topic; **conference:** conversation
65. **for:** because of; **urging it:** i.e., talking about it urgently
66. **board:** i.e., mealtimes; **fed:** i.e., ate
67. **Alone:** i.e., when we were alone
68. **glancèd:** i.e., alluded to
69. **Still:** continually, constantly
71. **venom:** venomous, poisonous
77. **ill:** bad
78. **bred:** came into being
80. **sports:** pastimes, amusements
84. **her heels:** i.e., the heels of despair
85. **distemperatures:** illnesses; disturbances of the mind
87. **mad:** madden; **or man:** i.e., man
91. **demeaned himself:** behaved

A snail. (2.2.205)
From Thomas Trevelyon's pictorial commonplace book (1608).

ADRIANA          And in assemblies too.

ABBESS   Ay, but not enough.

ADRIANA
It was the copy of our conference.
In bed he slept not for my urging it;                     65
At board he fed not for my urging it.
Alone, it was the subject of my theme;
In company I often glancèd it.
Still did I tell him it was vile and bad.

ABBESS
And thereof came it that the man was mad.          70
The venom clamors of a jealous woman
Poisons more deadly than a mad dog's tooth.
It seems his sleeps were hindered by thy railing,
And thereof comes it that his head is light.
Thou sayst his meat was sauced with thy             75
    upbraidings.
Unquiet meals make ill digestions.
Thereof the raging fire of fever bred,
And what's a fever but a fit of madness?
Thou sayest his sports were hindered by thy brawls.  80
Sweet recreation barred, what doth ensue
But moody and dull melancholy,
Kinsman to grim and comfortless despair,
And at her heels a huge infectious troop
Of pale distemperatures and foes to life?           85
In food, in sport, and life-preserving rest
To be disturbed would mad or man or beast.
The consequence is, then, thy jealous fits
Hath scared thy husband from the use of wits.

LUCIANA
She never reprehended him but mildly                 90
When he demeaned himself rough, rude, and
    wildly.—
Why bear you these rebukes and answer not?

94. **betray me:** i.e., reveal my real character

99. **privilege him:** i.e., grant him immunity, protect him

101. **assaying:** attempting

103. **Diet:** provide healthful food (for him in); **office:** duty; or, function (Adriana may here refer to the promise made at the time of marriage "to have and to hold . . . in sickness and in health.")

104. **attorney:** agent, deputy

107. **approvèd:** tested, proved

109. **formal:** sane

110. **parcel:** constituent part

111. **my order:** i.e., the religious community of which I am a member

114. **ill:** badly; **beseem:** suit

**ADRIANA**
She did betray me to my own reproof.—
Good people, enter and lay hold on him.                    95
**ABBESS**
No, not a creature enters in my house.
**ADRIANA**
Then let your servants bring my husband forth.
**ABBESS**
Neither. He took this place for sanctuary,
And it shall privilege him from your hands
Till I have brought him to his wits again          100
Or lose my labor in assaying it.
**ADRIANA**
I will attend my husband, be his nurse,
Diet his sickness, for it is my office
And will have no attorney but myself;
And therefore let me have him home with me.        105
**ABBESS**
Be patient, for I will not let him stir
Till I have used the approvèd means I have,
With wholesome syrups, drugs, and holy prayers,
To make of him a formal man again.
It is a branch and parcel of mine oath,            110
A charitable duty of my order.
Therefore depart and leave him here with me.
**ADRIANA**
I will not hence and leave my husband here;
And ill it doth beseem your holiness
To separate the husband and the wife.              115
**ABBESS**
Be quiet and depart. Thou shalt not have him.
**LUCIANA,** ⌜*to Adriana*⌝
Complain unto the Duke of this indignity.
**ADRIANA**
Come, go. I will fall prostrate at his feet
And never rise until my tears and prayers

121. **perforce:** forcibly
122. **By this:** i.e., by this time; **dial:** i.e., clock
123. **Anon:** soon
125. **sorry:** painful, distressful
133 SD. **bare head:** i.e., bareheaded
136. **so much we tender him:** i.e., I have thus much pity or compassion for him; or, I offer him this much
142. **important letters:** i.e., importunate letters, or letters urging me (to marry him); **ill:** evil

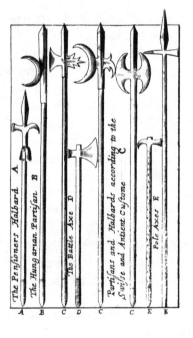

Halberds and partisans. (5.1.191)
From Louis de Gaya, *A treatise of the arms* . . . (1678).

Have won his grace to come in person hither                    120
And take perforce my husband from the Abbess.
⌐SECOND¬ MERCHANT
By this, I think, the dial points at five.
Anon, I'm sure, the Duke himself in person
Comes this way to the melancholy vale,
The place of ⌐death¬ and sorry execution                       125
Behind the ditches of the abbey here.
ANGELO  Upon what cause?
⌐SECOND¬ MERCHANT
To see a reverend Syracusian merchant,
Who put unluckily into this bay
Against the laws and statutes of this town,                    130
Beheaded publicly for his offense.
ANGELO
See where they come. We will behold his death.
LUCIANA, ⌐*to Adriana*¬
Kneel to the Duke before he pass the abbey.

*Enter the Duke of Ephesus, and* ⌐*Egeon*¬ *the Merchant*
*of Syracuse, bare head, with the Headsman*
*and other Officers.*

DUKE
Yet once again proclaim it publicly,
If any friend will pay the sum for him,                        135
He shall not die; so much we tender him.
ADRIANA, ⌐*kneeling*¬
Justice, most sacred duke, against the Abbess.
DUKE
She is a virtuous and a reverend lady.
It cannot be that she hath done thee wrong.
ADRIANA
May it please your Grace, Antipholus my husband,              140
Who I made lord of me and all I had
At your important letters, this ill day
A most outrageous fit of madness took him,

144. **That:** i.e., so that; **desp'rately:** recklessly, outrageously

145. **bondman:** i.e., bondsman, slave; **all:** quite

146. **displeasure:** wrong, offense

148. **rage:** madness

150. **Whilst . . . I went:** i.e., while I went to make arrangements for settling the wrongs

152. **Anon:** soon; **wot:** know; **strong:** powerful (i.e., performed with muscular strength)

155. **ireful passion:** irate emotions

156. **bent on us:** i.e., intent on us; or, perhaps, turned against us

161. **suffer:** allow

162. **Nor send:** i.e., nor will she send

163. **command:** order

164. **help:** relief, cure, remedy

165. **Long since:** i.e., a long time ago

166. **engaged:** pledged

171. **determine:** settle, decide

172. **shift:** escape

174. **a-row:** i.e., one after the other

174–82. **bound the doctor . . . conjurer:** See longer note, pages 168–69.

That desp'rately he hurried through the street,
With him his bondman, all as mad as he,                    145
Doing displeasure to the citizens
By rushing in their houses, bearing thence
Rings, jewels, anything his rage did like.
Once did I get him bound and sent him home
Whilst to take order for the wrongs I went          150
That here and there his fury had committed.
Anon, I wot not by what strong escape,
He broke from those that had the guard of him,
And with his mad attendant and himself,
Each one with ireful passion, with drawn swords,   155
Met us again and, madly bent on us,
Chased us away, till raising of more aid,
We came again to bind them. Then they fled
Into this abbey, whither we pursued them,
And here the Abbess shuts the gates on us           160
And will not suffer us to fetch him out,
Nor send him forth that we may bear him hence.
Therefore, most gracious duke, with thy command
Let him be brought forth and borne hence for help.

DUKE
Long since, thy husband served me in my wars,      165
And I to thee engaged a prince's word,
When thou didst make him master of thy bed,
To do him all the grace and good I could.
Go, some of you, knock at the abbey gate,
And bid the Lady Abbess come to me.                170
I will determine this before I stir.     ⌜*Adriana rises.*⌝

*Enter a Messenger.*

⌜MESSENGER⌝
O mistress, mistress, shift and save yourself.
My master and his man are both broke loose,
Beaten the maids a-row, and bound the doctor,

178. **puddled mire:** i.e., foul slush

180. **nicks him like a fool:** perhaps, cuts his hair so that he looks like a professional Fool (See below.)

181. **sure:** i.e., surely; **present:** immediate

186. **have not breathed almost:** i.e., have hardly taken a breath

188. **scorch:** burn; or, perhaps, slash

191. **halberds:** military weapons that combine the spear with the battle-ax (See page 138.)

194. **Even now:** i.e., just now; **housed him in:** i.e., drove him into

198. **bestrid thee:** i.e., stood straddling your fallen body

201. **dote:** lose my mind

Fool wearing a coxcomb. (3.1.43, 5.1.180)
From Desiderius Erasmus, *Moria[e] enkomion* . . . (1676).

Whose beard they have singed off with brands of      175
    fire,
And ever as it blazed they threw on him
Great pails of puddled mire to quench the hair.
My master preaches patience to him, and the while
His man with scissors nicks him like a fool;      180
And sure, unless you send some present help,
Between them they will kill the conjurer.

ADRIANA
Peace, fool. Thy master and his man are here,
And that is false thou dost report to us.

MESSENGER
Mistress, upon my life I tell you true.      185
I have not breathed almost since I did see it.
He cries for you and vows, if he can take you,
To scorch your face and to disfigure you.  *Cry within.*
Hark, hark, I hear him, mistress. Fly, begone!

DUKE
Come, stand by me. Fear nothing.—Guard with      190
    halberds.

*Enter Antipholus and Dromio of Ephesus.*

ADRIANA
Ay me, it is my husband. Witness you
That he is borne about invisible.
Even now we housed him in the abbey here,
And now he's there, past thought of human reason.      195

ANTIPHOLUS OF EPHESUS
Justice, most gracious duke. O, grant me justice,
Even for the service that long since I did thee
When I bestrid thee in the wars and took
Deep scars to save thy life. Even for the blood
That then I lost for thee, now grant me justice.      200

EGEON, ⌜*aside*⌝
Unless the fear of death doth make me dote,
I see my son Antipholus and Dromio.

205. **abusèd:** misused, wronged
206. **Even in . . . injury:** i.e., in the most injurious manner possible
208. **shameless:** i.e., shamelessly
209. **Discover:** reveal
211. **harlots:** rogues, knaves
214–15. **So befall . . . withal:** i.e., I stake the fate of my soul on (my truthfulness in reporting) the falseness of what he claims about me
216. **on night:** i.e., at night
218. **are both forsworn:** have both sworn falsely, have perjured themselves
219. **chargeth:** accuses
220. **advisèd:** i.e., heedful of
222. **heady-rash:** i.e., headstrong and rash
225. **packed with her:** i.e., a confederate of hers
230. **he:** i.e., Angelo, the goldsmith

ANTIPHOLUS OF EPHESUS
    Justice, sweet prince, against that woman there,
    She whom thou gav'st to me to be my wife,
    That hath abusèd and dishonored me                          205
    Even in the strength and height of injury.
    Beyond imagination is the wrong
    That she this day hath shameless thrown on me.
DUKE
    Discover how, and thou shalt find me just.
ANTIPHOLUS OF EPHESUS
    This day, great duke, she shut the doors upon me            210
    While she with harlots feasted in my house.
DUKE
    A grievous fault.—Say, woman, didst thou so?
ADRIANA
    No, my good lord. Myself, he, and my sister
    Today did dine together. So befall my soul
    As this is false he burdens me withal.                      215
LUCIANA
    Ne'er may I look on day nor sleep on night
    But she tells to your Highness simple truth.
ANGELO
    O perjured woman!—They are both forsworn.
    In this the madman justly chargeth them.
ANTIPHOLUS OF EPHESUS
    My liege, I am advisèd what I say,                          220
    Neither disturbed with the effect of wine,
    Nor heady-rash provoked with raging ire,
    Albeit my wrongs might make one wiser mad.
    This woman locked me out this day from dinner.
    That goldsmith there, were he not packed with her,          225
    Could witness it, for he was with me then,
    Who parted with me to go fetch a chain,
    Promising to bring it to the Porpentine,
    Where Balthasar and I did dine together.
    Our dinner done and he not coming thither,                  230

236. **arrest . . . officer:** i.e., have an officer arrest me

239. **fairly I bespoke:** I courteously requested

246. **anatomy:** skeleton

246, 247. **mountebank, juggler:** See note to 1.2.100.

248. **sharp-looking:** hungry-looking

250. **took on him as:** i.e., professed to be; or, assumed the part of (For a possible echo of Acts 19.13, see longer note to 5.1.174–82.) **conjurer:** exorcist

253. **possessed:** See note to 4.4.58.

255. **dankish:** wet

262. **witness:** attest, bear witness

A malt-horse. (3.1.43)
From Jacques Besson, *Theatrum instrumentorum et machinarum* . . . (1578).

I went to seek him. In the street I met him,
And in his company that gentleman.
⌈*He points to Second Merchant.*⌉
There did this perjured goldsmith swear me down
That I this day of him received the chain,
Which, God He knows, I saw not; for the which        235
He did arrest me with an officer.
I did obey and sent my peasant home
For certain ducats. He with none returned.
Then fairly I bespoke the officer
To go in person with me to my house.        240
By th' way we met
My wife, her sister, and a rabble more
Of vile confederates. Along with them
They brought one Pinch, a hungry, lean-faced
       villain,        245
A mere anatomy, a mountebank,
A threadbare juggler, and a fortune-teller,
A needy, hollow-eyed, sharp-looking wretch,
A living dead man. This pernicious slave,
Forsooth, took on him as a conjurer,        250
And, gazing in mine eyes, feeling my pulse,
And with no face (as 'twere) outfacing me,
Cries out I was possessed. Then all together
They fell upon me, bound me, bore me thence,
And in a dark and dankish vault at home        255
There left me and my man, both bound together,
Till gnawing with my teeth my bonds in sunder,
I gained my freedom and immediately
Ran hither to your Grace, whom I beseech
To give me ample satisfaction        260
For these deep shames and great indignities.
ANGELO
My lord, in truth, thus far I witness with him:
That he dined not at home, but was locked out.

264. **of thee:** i.e., from you

269. **forswore it:** denied it

277. **intricate impeach:** i.e., involved accusation

278. **have drunk of Circe's cup:** i.e., have been transformed (Circe, in Homer's *Odyssey*, changed men into animals through a potion given them in her cup. See below, and longer note, page 169.)

280. **coldly:** dispassionately

283. **saying:** utterance

Circe. (5.1.278)
From Geoffrey Whitney, *A choice of emblemes . . .* (1586)

DUKE
But had he such a chain of thee or no?

ANGELO
He had, my lord, and when he ran in here,               265
These people saw the chain about his neck.

⌜SECOND⌝ MERCHANT, ⌜*to Antipholus of Ephesus*⌝
Besides, I will be sworn these ears of mine
Heard you confess you had the chain of him
After you first forswore it on the mart,
And thereupon I drew my sword on you,                  270
And then you fled into this abbey here,
From whence I think you are come by miracle.

ANTIPHOLUS OF EPHESUS
I never came within these abbey walls,
Nor ever didst thou draw thy sword on me.
I never saw the chain, so help me heaven,              275
And this is false you burden me withal.

DUKE
Why, what an intricate impeach is this!
I think you all have drunk of Circe's cup.
If here you housed him, here he would have been.
If he were mad, he would not plead so coldly.          280
⌜*To Adriana.*⌝ You say he dined at home; the
    goldsmith here
Denies that saying. ⌜*To Dromio of Ephesus.*⌝ Sirrah,
    what say you?

DROMIO OF EPHESUS, ⌜*pointing to the Courtesan*⌝
Sir, he dined with her there at the Porpentine.        285

COURTESAN
He did, and from my finger snatched that ring.

ANTIPHOLUS OF EPHESUS, ⌜*showing a ring*⌝
'Tis true, my liege, this ring I had of her.

DUKE, ⌜*to Courtesan*⌝
Saw'st thou him enter at the abbey here?

COURTESAN
As sure, my liege, as I do see your Grace.

291. **mated:** confounded, stupefied

293. **Haply:** perchance, perhaps (Here the word reflects its connections with "happily.")

302. **Ourselves . . . by you:** i.e., you make us recall our past situation

305. **look you strange on me:** i.e., look at me as if we were strangers

308. **careful hours:** i.e., hours filled with care; **deformèd:** i.e., deforming; or, perhaps, deformed because it is the ancient hand of Father Time

309. **defeatures:** deformities, disfigurements

DUKE
Why, this is strange.—Go call the Abbess hither.    290
*Exit one to the Abbess.*
I think you are all mated or stark mad.
EGEON
Most mighty duke, vouchsafe me speak a word.
Haply I see a friend will save my life
And pay the sum that may deliver me.
DUKE
Speak freely, Syracusian, what thou wilt.    295
EGEON, ⌐*to Antipholus of Ephesus*⌐
Is not your name, sir, called Antipholus?
And is not that your bondman Dromio?
DROMIO OF EPHESUS
Within this hour I was his bondman, sir,
But he, I thank him, gnawed in two my cords.
Now am I Dromio, and his man, unbound.    300
EGEON
I am sure you both of you remember me.
DROMIO OF EPHESUS
Ourselves we do remember, sir, by you,
For lately we were bound as you are now.
You are not Pinch's patient, are you, sir?
EGEON, ⌐*to Antipholus of Ephesus*⌐
Why look you strange on me? You know me well.    305
ANTIPHOLUS OF EPHESUS
I never saw you in my life till now.
EGEON
O, grief hath changed me since you saw me last,
And careful hours with time's deformèd hand
Have written strange defeatures in my face.
But tell me yet, dost thou not know my voice?    310
ANTIPHOLUS OF EPHESUS    Neither.
EGEON    Dromio, nor thou?
DROMIO OF EPHESUS    No, trust me, sir, nor I.

318. **extremity:** extreme severity or rigor

321. **my feeble key of untuned cares:** i.e., my voice (The general sense here is of the voice as an instrument that plays feebly and out of tune, aged by anxiety and sorrow.)

322. **grainèd:** rough and wrinkled (like leather)

323. **sap-consuming . . . snow:** i.e., a white beard **sap-consuming:** i.e., youth-destroying (The familiar equation of old age with winter is used again in line 324.)

325. **night of life:** i.e., old age

326. **wasting lamps:** i.e., dimming eyes

331. **since:** i.e., ago

EGEON  I am sure thou dost.

DROMIO OF EPHESUS  Ay, sir, but I am sure I do not, and    315
 whatsoever a man denies, you are now bound to
 believe him.

EGEON
 Not know my voice! O time's extremity,
 Hast thou so cracked and splitted my poor tongue
 In seven short years that here my only son          320
 Knows not my feeble key of untuned cares?
 Though now this grainèd face of mine be hid
 In sap-consuming winter's drizzled snow,
 And all the conduits of my blood froze up,
 Yet hath my night of life some memory,              325
 My wasting lamps some fading glimmer left,
 My dull deaf ears a little use to hear.
 All these old witnesses—I cannot err—
 Tell me thou art my son Antipholus.

ANTIPHOLUS OF EPHESUS
 I never saw my father in my life.                   330

EGEON
 But seven years since, in Syracusa, boy,
 Thou know'st we parted. But perhaps, my son,
 Thou sham'st to acknowledge me in misery.

ANTIPHOLUS OF EPHESUS
 The Duke and all that know me in the city
 Can witness with me that it is not so.              335
 I ne'er saw Syracusa in my life.

DUKE
 I tell thee, Syracusian, twenty years
 Have I been patron to Antipholus,
 During which time he ne'er saw Syracusa.
 I see thy age and dangers make thee dote.           340

*Enter* ⌐Emilia⌐ *the Abbess, with Antipholus* ⌐of⌐
*Syracuse and Dromio* ⌐of⌐ *Syracuse.*

343. **genius:** attendant spirit (here imagined as being the exact image of the person)

345. **deciphers them:** makes them out, i.e., distinguishes between them

354. **at a burden:** i.e., in a single birth

358. **Antipholus':** i.e., Antipholuses

359. **one in semblance:** i.e., one person in their looks

360. **urging of:** i.e., story about, account of (Pointing out that Emilia has not yet mentioned **her wrack at sea,** some editors move this speech by the Duke to follow Emilia's next speech. However, in that speech, Emilia does not mention the **wrack,** only the rescue.)

Testing gold on a touchstone. (2.1.115–16)
From George Wither, *A collection of emblemes . . .* (1635).

ABBESS
Most mighty duke, behold a man much wronged.
                                    *All gather to see them.*
ADRIANA
I see two husbands, or mine eyes deceive me.
DUKE
One of these men is genius to the other.
And so, of these, which is the natural man
And which the spirit? Who deciphers them?          345
DROMIO OF SYRACUSE
I, sir, am Dromio. Command him away.
DROMIO OF EPHESUS
I, sir, am Dromio. Pray, let me stay.
ANTIPHOLUS OF SYRACUSE
Egeon art thou not, or else his ghost?
DROMIO OF SYRACUSE
O, my old master.—Who hath bound him here?
ABBESS
Whoever bound him, I will loose his bonds          350
And gain a husband by his liberty.—
Speak, old Egeon, if thou be'st the man
That hadst a wife once called Emilia,
That bore thee at a burden two fair sons.
O, if thou be'st the same Egeon, speak,          355
And speak unto the same Emilia.
DUKE
Why, here begins his morning story right:
These two Antipholus', these two so like,
And these two Dromios, one in semblance—
Besides her urging of her wrack at sea—          360
These are the parents to these children,
Which accidentally are met together.
EGEON
If I dream not, thou art Emilia.
If thou art she, tell me, where is that son
That floated with thee on the fatal raft?          365

368. **rude:** uncivilized, rough

388. **leisure:** opportunity; **make good:** i.e., prove true

Fortune. (1.1.105)
From George Wither, *A collection of emblemes . . .* (1635).

ABBESS
By men of Epidamium he and I
And the twin Dromio all were taken up;
But by and by rude fishermen of Corinth
By force took Dromio and my son from them,
And me they left with those of Epidamium.          370
What then became of them I cannot tell;
I to this fortune that you see me in.
DUKE, ⌜*to Antipholus of Syracuse*⌝
Antipholus, thou cam'st from Corinth first.
ANTIPHOLUS OF SYRACUSE
No, sir, not I. I came from Syracuse.
DUKE
Stay, stand apart. I know not which is which.          375
ANTIPHOLUS OF EPHESUS
I came from Corinth, my most gracious lord.
DROMIO OF EPHESUS    And I with him.
ANTIPHOLUS OF EPHESUS
Brought to this town by that most famous warrior
Duke Menaphon, your most renownèd uncle.
ADRIANA
Which of you two did dine with me today?          380
ANTIPHOLUS OF SYRACUSE
I, gentle mistress.
ADRIANA                    And are not you my husband?
ANTIPHOLUS OF EPHESUS    No, I say nay to that.
ANTIPHOLUS OF SYRACUSE
And so do I, yet did she call me so,
And this fair gentlewoman, her sister here,          385
Did call me brother. ⌜*To Luciana.*⌝ What I told you
   then
I hope I shall have leisure to make good,
If this be not a dream I see and hear.
ANGELO, ⌜*turning to Antipholus of Syracuse*⌝
That is the chain, sir, which you had of me.          390

398. **them me:** i.e., them to me
399. **still:** constantly
403. **need:** i.e., be necessary
408. **at large:** i.e., fully, at length
410. **sympathizèd:** i.e., shared in by all equally
413. **in travail:** in the labor of childbirth (The childbirth metaphor continues in lines 414–15 and 419.)

A christening. (5.1.418)
From [Richard Day,] *A booke of christian prayers* . . . (1578).

ANTIPHOLUS OF SYRACUSE
I think it be, sir. I deny it not.
ANTIPHOLUS OF EPHESUS, ⌈*to Angelo*⌉
And you, sir, for this chain arrested me.
ANGELO
I think I did, sir. I deny it not.
ADRIANA, ⌈*to Antipholus of Ephesus*⌉
I sent you money, sir, to be your bail
By Dromio, but I think he brought it not.                395
DROMIO OF EPHESUS   No, none by me.
ANTIPHOLUS OF SYRACUSE, ⌈*to Adriana*⌉
This purse of ducats I received from you,
And Dromio my man did bring them me.
I see we still did meet each other's man,
And I was ta'en for him, and he for me,                400
And thereupon these errors are arose.
ANTIPHOLUS OF EPHESUS, ⌈*to the Duke*⌉
These ducats pawn I for my father here.
DUKE
It shall not need. Thy father hath his life.
COURTESAN, ⌈*to Antipholus of Ephesus*⌉
Sir, I must have that diamond from you.
ANTIPHOLUS OF EPHESUS
There, take it, and much thanks for my good cheer.   405
ABBESS
Renownèd duke, vouchsafe to take the pains
To go with us into the abbey here
And hear at large discoursèd all our fortunes,
And all that are assembled in this place
That by this sympathizèd one day's error               410
Have suffered wrong. Go, keep us company,
And we shall make full satisfaction.—
Thirty-three years have I but gone in travail
Of you, my sons, and till this present hour
My heavy burden ⌈ne'er⌉ deliverèd.—                   415
The Duke, my husband, and my children both,

417. **the calendars of their nativity:** i.e., the twin Dromios (Because they were born at the same time as their masters, they, like calendars, fix the date of their masters' births.)

418. **gossips' feast:** i.e., a baptismal or christening feast **gossips':** i.e., godparents' (See page 158.)

420. **gossip:** take part in

421. **stuff:** i.e., luggage

422. **embarked:** put on board a ship

423. **lay at host:** i.e., were put up at the hostel or inn

428. **kitchened me:** perhaps, entertained me in the kitchen

429. **sister:** i.e., sister-in-law

430. **Methinks:** i.e., it seems to me; **glass:** looking glass, mirror

432. **Will you walk in:** The response in line 433 shows that Dromio of Ephesus gestures to his brother to precede him through the door.

435. **try:** test, determine

436. **draw cuts:** i.e., draw lots; **signior:** Usually modernized to "senior," this Folio spelling, **signior,** may indicate a term of respect such as would be given to one's social superior, or, here, one's elder brother.

And you, the calendars of their nativity,
Go to a gossips' feast, and go with me.
After so long grief, such nativity!

DUKE
With all my heart I'll gossip at this feast.                    420
                    *All exit except the two Dromios*
                    *and ⌐the⌐ two brothers ⌐Antipholus.⌐*

DROMIO OF SYRACUSE, ⌐*to Antipholus of Ephesus*⌐
Master, shall I fetch your stuff from shipboard?

ANTIPHOLUS OF EPHESUS
Dromio, what stuff of mine hast thou embarked?

DROMIO OF SYRACUSE
Your goods that lay at host, sir, in the Centaur.

ANTIPHOLUS OF SYRACUSE, ⌐*to Antipholus of Ephesus*⌐
He speaks to me.—I am your master, Dromio.
Come, go with us. We'll look to that anon.                    425
Embrace thy brother there. Rejoice with him.
                    ⌐*The brothers Antipholus*⌐ *exit.*

DROMIO OF SYRACUSE
There is a fat friend at your master's house
That kitchened me for you today at dinner.
She now shall be my sister, not my wife.

DROMIO OF EPHESUS
Methinks you are my glass, and not my brother.                430
I see by you I am a sweet-faced youth.
Will you walk in to see their gossiping?

DROMIO OF SYRACUSE    Not I, sir. You are my elder.

DROMIO OF EPHESUS    That's a question. How shall we
    try it?                                                   435

DROMIO OF SYRACUSE    We'll draw cuts for the signior.
    Till then, lead thou first.

DROMIO OF EPHESUS    Nay, then, thus:
We came into the world like brother and brother,
And now let's go hand in hand, not one before                 440
    another.
                                        *They exit.*

# Longer Notes

**1.1.0 SD. Ephesus, Syracuse:** The travels of St. Paul, recounted in the Acts of the Apostles, associated **Ephesus** prominently with witchcraft and sorcery. **Syracuse** was famous in classical times as a major Greek settlement. See Acts 18–20 for an account of Paul's two-year stay in **Ephesus** and Acts 28:12 for his visit to **Syracuse.**

**1.1.8. guilders:** The play uses the terms *guilders, marks, ducats, angels, pounds,* and *pence* indiscriminately to refer to money.

**1.1.9. sealed his rigorous statutes with their bloods:** Official documents are normally **sealed** with red wax; here, the dead merchants have figuratively affixed seals of blood to Syracuse's statutes.

**1.1.11. mortal and intestine jars: Intestine** means "civil" or "internal," and suggests that the conflict between Syracuse and Ephesus, historically Greek city-states, might be perceived as a kind of civil war.

**1.1.41. Epidamium:** i.e., Epidamnus, a port on the Adriatic Sea and the setting of Plautus's play *Menaechmi,* the primary source of *The Comedy of Errors*

**1.1.52. but by names:** We learn later that Egeon's sons have the same name, "Antipholus." At line 128, Egeon says that the twin that remained with him "retained" the lost twin's name. This suggests that Egeon, like his counterpart in Plautus's play, may be imagined to have renamed the son he saved after the son he lost.

**1.1.79. small spare mast:** Sir Henry Mainwaring's *The Sea-mans Dictionary: or an exposition and demonstration of all the Parts and Things belonging to a Shippe* (London, 1644) defines a jury-rigged mast, or "jury-mast," as a temporary mast put up when the main or foremast has blown away: "When by some occasion of storm, or fight, we have lost either the fore-mast or main-mast, we do reserve (if it be possible) the main or fore-yard; which we put down into the step [i.e., 'that piece of timber which is made fast to the keelson wherein the main-mast doth stand'] of the mast . . . which fitting with sails and ropes . . . we make a shift with a steer and govern the Ship" (pp. 55–56, 103).

**1.1.132–34. Five summers have I spent in farthest Greece,/Roaming clean through the bounds of Asia,/ And, coasting homeward, came to Ephesus. . . . :** The influence of St. Paul's journeys to, and long sojourn in, Ephesus is apparent in these lines. In Acts 13–20, which describe Paul's three journeys through **Greece** and **Asia,** the word **Asia** is used much as we would use "Asia Minor," to refer to the peninsula at the western tip of the continent, bordered by the Aegean Sea to the west, the Mediterranean to the south, the Black (or Pontic) Sea to the North, and the Euphrates River to the east. (This is essentially the area of the first Roman province to the east of the Aegean, also called **Asia.**) As the *Encyclopedia Britannica* (11th ed.) notes, "[Even] after the word Asia had acquired its larger sense it was still specially used by the Greeks to designate the country around Ephesus." That the Book of Acts uses the term **Asia** to mean the peninsula that includes **Ephesus** is indicated by such statements as this one referring to Paul's preaching in Ephesus: "This continued for two years, so that all the residents of Asia heard the word of the Lord" (Acts 19.10). Shakespeare uses **Asia** in this more restricted sense in *Antony and Cleopatra* 1.2: "Labenus . . . hath with his Parthian force / Extended [i.e., captured] Asia; from Euphrates / His conquering banner shook, from Syria / To Lydia, and to Ionia. . . ."

It has also been suggested that Egeon's travels echo those of the Wandering Twin in Plautus's *Menaechmi*, who tells of six years of roaming through "Istria, Hispania, Massilia, Illyria, all the upper sea, all High Greece, all haven towns in Italy."

**1.2.0 SD. Antipholus of Syracuse:** In the Folio, Antipholus of Syracuse is called "Antipholis Erotes" and at 2.2.0 SD he is called "Antipholis Errotis." Both *Erotes* and *Errotis* are nonsense words, but scholars have suggested that they may be scribal or compositorial corruptions of the Latin words *erraticus* or *errans*, both meaning "wandering"—an appropriate designation for Antipholus of Syracuse, whom his father has already described as wandering in search of the other Antipholus. The Folio once refers to this other Antipholus, whom it usually names Antipholus of Ephesus in stage directions, as "Antipholis Sereptus" (2.1.0 SD). *Sereptus*, like *Erotes* and *Errotis*, is nonsense, but again scholars have offered a suggestion about what might lie behind it: the word *surreptus*, meaning "snatched away," and possibly alluding to the way that this Antipholus was, according to his father Egeon, "taken up / By fishermen of Corinth" (1.1.110–11).

**2.1.60. cuckold:** The word *cuckold* comes from the name of the cuckoo, a bird which does not build a nest but instead leaves its eggs for other birds to hatch and feed. The association of cuckolds with horns growing from the forehead goes back to ancient times and may originate with the early and prevalent practice of "grafting the spurs of a castrated cock on the root of the excised comb, where they grew and became horns, sometimes of several inches long" (OED *horn* 7a.)

**2.1.112. Would that alone o' love he would detain:** This line has been much debated and emended. Many editors follow the Second Folio and print "Would that alone, alone he would detain." In the First Folio reading, which we retain, the line means, perhaps, "would that were the only part of his love that he kept (from me)."

**2.1.114–18. I see . . . shame:** These difficult lines are printed in the Folio as follows:

> I see the Iewell best enamaled
> Will loose his beautie: yet the gold bides still
> That others touch, and often touching will,
> Where gold and no man that hath a name,
> By falshood and corruption doth it shame.

Editors are agreed that the lines are textually corrupt, and, beginning in 1733, many have attempted to emend them. Our version of the lines adopts the editorial changes in line 117 of "Where" to "Wear" and "and" to "yet," emendations that help make some sense of the lines and that allow them to continue Adriana's attack on men and her lament for her fading beauty. Even with these emendations, the logic of lines 115–17 ("Yet the gold bides still / That others touch, and often touching will / Wear gold") is quite puzzling. Other popular emendations include: changing "and" (line 116) to "yet" and changing "By" (line 118) to "But."

**2.2.47. flouting:** Dromio's question, "Why am I beaten?" and Antipholus's answer, "For flouting me," echo the familiar biblical story (Numbers 22.21–34) of Balaam and his ass. The ass, seeing an angel barring Balaam's way, refuses to go forward and is three times severely beaten. God allows the ass to speak, and she asks Balaam: "'What have I done unto thee, that thou hast smitten me these three times?' And Balaam said unto the ass, 'Because thou hast mocked me. . . .' And the ass said unto Balaam, 'Am not I thine ass, upon which thou hast ridden ever since I was thine unto this day?'" This dialogue also seems echoed in 4.4.32–35, where Dromio of Ephesus, beaten by his master, says "I am an ass, indeed. . . . I have served him from the hour of my nativity to this instant, and have nothing at his hands for my service but blows."

2.2.157. **distained:** This word normally means to stain, defile, or deprive of color or splendor. It clearly cannot mean any of these in this context. Editors frequently change the word to "unstained." However, John Palsgrave's *Lesclarcissement de la langue Francoyse*, 1530, sig. 3E5v.) defines the word *distain* as "change the color of a thing." We therefore suggest the meaning "clear of stain (literally, changed in color)."

3.2.47. **mermaid:** In classical mythology, the Sirens (often equated with mermaids) used their alluring songs to entice sailors to their deaths on the rocks near their island. In the most famous mythological encounter with the Sirens, Odysseus has himself tied to the mast of his ship (after stopping up the ears of his sailors with wax) so that he can safely hear the songs of the Sirens as the ship passes their island (Homer's *Odyssey* XII).

4.2.37. **Tartar limbo:** This designation for a prison appears to combine references to (1) Tartarus, the region below Hades in Greek mythology; (2) Tartars (i.e., Tatars, members of Mongolian tribes); (3) **limbo**, the region that borders hell in early Christian theology where, e.g., the souls of unbaptized infants go.

**4.2.40. fairy:** Although often emended by editors to *fury*, there are clear indications elsewhere in Shakespeare's period that fairies might well be classed with fiends. See, e.g., this list from Thomas Thomas's 1615 Latin-English dictionary: "Hobgoblins, or nightwalking spirits, black bugs, fairies."

**4.3.13–14. picture of old Adam new-appareled:** This much-disputed line begins a series of quibbling descriptions of the officer, extending through line 34, and including many probable puns. The **picture of old Adam** may link the officer with Adam through the fact that Adam was naked (in the **buff**) before the Fall and that the officer is dressed in buff; or, since "in the buff" as an expression for nakedness is not recorded until 1602, about a decade after this play is thought to have been written, Adam and the officer may be linked through Adam's "coats of **skin**" worn after the Fall (Genesis 3.21), since the officer is dressed in buff-leather. The officer's leather coat is alluded to again in lines 18–19, where he is said to be dressed in **the calf's skin that was killed for the Prodigal,** an allusion to the Prodigal Son (Luke 15.11–32), whose father killed a calf to celebrate the son's return.

There is probably a buried pun in **new-appareled,** which can mean "in a new suit or a new case," with puns on "suit" and "case" as legal suit or case.

**5.1.174–82. bound the doctor . . . conjurer:** This punishment of the exorcist is reminiscent of an incident in Ephesus described in Acts 19.13–16. There fraudulent exorcists "took upon them to call over them which had evil spirits" and attempted to exorcise a devil from a possessed man; when the evil spirit determined that the exorcists were impostors, "the man in whom the evil spirit was leaped on them, and overcame them, and prevailed against them, so that they fled out of that house naked and wounded."

5.1.278. **have drunk of Circe's cup:** In Homer's *Odyssey*, Book X, Odysseus tells how he discovers his men transformed into swine by the goddess Circe. He describes his meeting with her: "She made me a mixture in a golden cup to drink, / And put in a drug, devising evil in her heart" (Albert Cook translation). Because Hermes has given Odysseus a charm to protect him from "Circe's cup," Odysseus is not affected by her drug and he saves his transformed men.

# Textual Notes

The reading of the present text appears to the left of the square bracket. Unless otherwise noted, the reading to the left of the bracket is from **F**, the First Folio text (upon which this edition is based). The earliest sources of readings not in **F** are indicated as follows: **F2** is the Second Folio of 1632; **F3** is the Third Folio of 1663–64; **F4** is the Fourth Folio of 1685; **Ed.** is an earlier editor of Shakespeare, beginning with Rowe in 1709. No sources are given for emendations of punctuation or for corrections of obvious typographical errors, like turned letters that produce no known word. **SD** means stage direction; **SP** means speech prefix; **uncorr.** means the first or uncorrected state of the First Folio; **corr.** means the second or corrected state of the First Folio; ~ stands in place of a word already quoted before the square bracket; ʌ indicates the omission of a punctuation mark.

**1.1**    1 *and hereafter in this scene.* SP EGEON] Ed.;
         *Marchant* (*Mer.*, *Merch.*)F
    17. at Syracusian] Ed.; at any *Siracusian* F
    42. the] Ed.; he F
    55. burden, male ʌ twins,] ~ ʌ ~, ~ ʌ F
    60. agreed.] ~, F
    75. was, . . . none:] ~: ( . . . ~) F
    102. upon] Ed.; vp F
    116. bark] F2; backe F
    123. thee] F2; they F
    144. princes, would they,] ~ ʌ ~ ~ ʌ F
    151. life] Ed.; helpe F

171

**1.2**     0. SD *Antipholus of Syracuse*] Ed.; *Antipholis Erotes* F (*Erotes*, an error, perhaps for *Errans*, or *Erraticus*, referring to Antipholus's wanderings) *First*] Ed.; *a* F

    1. SP FIRST MERCHANT] Ed.; *Mer.* F

    4. arrival] F2; a riuall F

    9 *and hereafter.* SP ANTIPHOLUS OF SYRACUSE] Ed.; *Ant., Anti., Antiph., An.* F, *except at* 3.2.31, 4.4.158, *and* 5.1.348–424, *where* F *has* "*S. Ant.,*" "*S. Anti.,*" *and* 2.2.14 *(See textual note.)*

    15. travel] F (trauaile)

    17, 2.2.167, 3.2.83, 87–171, 4.1.87, 4.2.32, 4.4.162. SP DROMIO OF SYRACUSE] Ed.; *Dro., Drom.* F

    24, 32. SP FIRST MERCHANT] Ed.; *E. Mar.* F

    32. SD *He exits*] this ed.; *Exeunt* F

    40. them, unhappy, lose] F2; them (vnhappie a) loose F

    43 *and hereafter with the exceptions listed in the note to line 2.1.81.* SP DROMIO OF EPHESUS] F *(E. Dro., E.D., E. Dr., E Drom., E. Dromio)*

    55. o'] F (a)

    67. clock] Ed.; cooke F

    75. from] F (frō)

    95. God's sake] F (God sake)

    97. SD *Dromio . . . exits.*] F *(Exeunt Dromio Ep.)*

    99. o'erraught] Ed.; ore-wrought F

**2.1**     0. SD *of Ephesus*] Ed.; *Sereptus* F (an error perhaps for *Surreptus*, referring to his being taken from his father in infancy)

    11. o'] F (a)

    12. ill] F2; thus F

43. SD *Dromio of Ephesus*] F *(Dromio Eph.)*
45. two hands] F (too hands)
63. thousand] F2 (1000.); hundred F
77. errand] F (arrant)
81, 84, 87, 4.1.21, 4.4.74–134, 5.1.302, 313. SP
    DROMIO OF EPHESUS] Ed.; *Dro.* F
91. loureth] F (lowreth)
96. wit?] ~, F
112. alone ˄] ~, F o'] F (a)
117. Wear] Ed.; Where F gold;] ~ ˄ F yet] Ed.;
    and F
120. weep ˄ what's left away,] ~ (~ ~ ~) F
121. SD *They exit*] this ed.; *Exit* F

**2.2**    0. SD *of Syracuse*] Ed.; *Errotis* F (See textual
    note to line 1.2.0.SD.)
1. SP ANTIPHOLUS OF SYRACUSE] F *(Ant.)*
3–4. out. | . . . report, |] ~ ˄ | . . . ~.| F
6. SD *of Syracuse*] F *(Siracusia)*
12. thou didst] F2; thou did didst F
13 *and hereafter (with the exceptions listed in
    note to line 1.2.17.)* SP DROMIO OF SYRA-
    CUSE] F *(S. Dro., S. Drom., S. Dromio)*
14. SP ANTIPHOLUS OF SYRACUSE] Ed.; *E. Ant.* F
17 *and hereafter in this scene.* SP ANTIPHOLUS OF
    SYRACUSE] Ed.; *Ant.* or *An.* F
23. SD *Dromio*] F *(Dro.)*
24. sake!] ~, F
29. hours.] ~, F
35. it? So ˄] F *corr.;* ~ ˄ ~? F *uncorr.*
37. head.] ~, F
88. men] Ed.; them F
106. one,] ~ ˄ F
107. tiring] Ed.; trying F
111. e'en] F (in)
132. me,] ~: F

133. That, . . . incorporate,] ~ ˄ . . . ~ ˄ F
147. off] F (of)
185. vine,] ~: F
186. stronger] F3; stranger F
197. offered] Ed.; free'd F
205. thou, Dromio] ~ ˄ ~ F
232. too] F (to)

**3.1**    31 *and hereafter.* SP ANTIPHOLUS OF EPHESUS]
Ed.; *Anti., Ant., An.* F, *except* 54, 4.1.22,
5.1.196, 203, 210, 220, 273, 287, 306,
376–422, *where* F *has* "E. Ant.," "E.
Anti.," "E. An.," *or* "Eph. Ant." (*as at*
3.1.1, 17, 22, 26)
58. not. Come] ~ ˄ ~ F
78. that's—When,] ~ ˄ ~? F
118. you] F2; your F
129–30. a feather] afether F
138. this:] ~ ˄ F
138. her] Ed.; ²your F
140. her] Ed.; your F
159. too,] ~ ˄ F
160. mean,] ~ ˄ F
168. there.] ~, F

**3.2**    0. SD *Luciana*] F2; *Iuliana* F
1. SP LUCIANA] Ed.; *Iulia.* F
4. building . . . ruinous] Ed.; buildings . . .
ruinate F
18. attaint] Ed.; attaine F
23. but] Ed.; not F
28. wife] F2; wise F
48. sister's] F2; sister F
51. bed] F2; bud F
51. them] Ed.; thee F
71. sister,] ~ ˄ F
97. reverend] F (reuerent)
112. sweats.] ~ ˄ F

119. and] Ed.; is F
138. chalky] chalkle F
149. carracks] F (Carrects)
162. curtal] F (Curtull)
174. high] F (hie)
182. Master] F (Mr)
194. now,] ~. F

**4.1**  1 *and hereafter.* SP SECOND MERCHANT] Ed.;
     *Mar.* F
   7 *and hereafter.* SP ANGELO] Ed.; *Gold.* F
   10. chain.] ~, F
   13. SD *Ephesus*] F (*Ephes.*)
   17. her] Ed.; their F
   35. town.] ~, F
   47. to] F (too)
   56. by me] Ed.; me by F
   86. SD *Syracuse*] F (*Sira.*)

**4.2**  6. Of] F2; Oh, F
   24. making,] ~ ˄ F
   31. SD *Dromio of Syracuse*] F (*S. Dromio*)
   39. One] F (On)
   44. alleys] F (allies); lands] F *corr.;* lans F
      *uncorr.*
   58. That] F2; Thus F
   75. he] Ed. (*as "a"*); I F
   81. SD *They exit*] Ed.; *Exit* F

**4.3**  0. SD *Syracuse*] F *corr.* (*Siracusia*); *Siracusian*
      F *uncorr.*
   1. SP ANTIPHOLUS OF SYRACUSE] F2 (*An. S.*);
      *omit* F
   11. SD *Syracuse*] F (*Sir.*)
   18. calf's] F (calues)
   41. *Delay*] F *corr.;* delay F *uncorr.*
   62. you] F2; *omit* F
   62. do,] ~ ˄ F
   68. all,] ~ ˄ F

82. SD *Antipholus . . . exit*] this ed.; *Exit* F

**4.4**    0. SD *Ephesus*] F (*Ephes.*)

7. SD *Ephesus*] F (*Eph.*)

48. SD *Dromio*] F (*Dro.*)

63. wert] F (wer't)

84. contraries] crontraries F

104. master] F (Mr)

112. SD *1 line earlier in* F

115. me? . . . thou,] ~, . . . ? F

138. SD *1 line later in* F

138. SD *Officer . . . remain*] F (*Manet Offic. Adri. Luci. Courtizan*)

153. SD *Syracuse . . . Syracuse*] *Siracusia . . . Sirac.* F

157. SD *Run all out*] *1 line earlier in* F; "*Exeunt omnes*" *printed here in its place in* F

**5.1**    5, 128. reverend] F (reuerent)

18. Besides] F (Beside)

33. God's] F (God)

71. woman ∧] ~, F

125. death] F3; depth F

142. letters,] ~ ∧ F

152. Anon, . . . not ∧] ~ ∧ . . . ~, F

179. master] F (Mr)

180. scissors] F (Cizers)

191. SD *4 lines later in* F; *Dromio*] *E. Dromio* F

195. human] F (humane)

201. SP EGEON] Ed.; *Mar. Fat.* F

253. all together] F (altogether)

290. SD *1 line later in* F

292 *and hereafter.* SP EGEON] Ed.; *Fa., Fath., Father, Fat.* F

318. extremity] e tremity F

328. err—] ~. F

340. SD *Dromio of Syracuse*] Ed.; *Dromio Sir.* F

409. place ˄] ~: F
415. ne'er] Ed.; are F
420. SD *except*] this ed.; *Manet* F
421. Master] F (Mast.)
426. SD *The brothers . . . exit*] *Exit.* F
441. SD *They exit*] this ed.; *Exennt* F

# The Comedy of Errors:
# A Modern Perspective
## Arthur F. Kinney

Reading *The Comedy of Errors* is a great deal of fun—
both up close, for the slapstick and the puns, and from
further back, where we can watch, sometimes in awe,
the sheer juggling act of events spinning out of mistaken
identity, certain that the whole improbable set of circumstances will come crashing down at any moment
and constantly surprised it does not. The form of this
play—among Shakespeare's earliest—represents the
round or catch, the most popular song forms of his time,
which took a single line or idea and kept building on it
through repetition and variation. At the same time,
reading *The Comedy of Errors* is, at least at first, a matter
of unending confusion; with twin Antipholuses and
Dromios on the stage, it is sometimes difficult to distinguish them, to keep the players straight and in proper
position and relationship to each other. The confusion
runs deep, beginning with the first scene.

Egeon's forced and painful narrative, the beginning of
the story, is torn by confusion (or, perhaps, by errors).
Egeon tells the Duke that he and Emilia can distinguish
their own sons only by name (52), yet the sons have the
same name, and the twins they buy to serve the sons also
share a single name (57). Emilia's "incessant weepings"
(70) cause Egeon to seek a way to save his family (74), yet
Emilia manages to do it (78–79) only to see the storm
dissipate (89). Now, in calm waters, the ship nevertheless crashes on "a mighty rock" (101). There are, of

course, still greater conundrums in this only apparently simple play. Why does Solinus pronounce a sentence and then suspend it for a day? Why don't the twins—at least Antipholus of Syracuse, who is, after all, searching for his twin—think that the presence of a twin might be the cause of the strange events he encounters? And how could his mother live for more than a decade in the same town as her son and his servant and not know of it? The play must have seemed especially appropriate for its presentation on December 28, 1594, at Gray's Inn in London, when, we are told, the night was also marked by such "Throngs and Tumults, Crowds and Outrages" that it soon became known as the "Night of Errors."

But these are not proper questions to ask of farce. From the widespread study of Plautus's farces in the Elizabethan grammar schools, many Elizabethan play-goers would know that this kind of play is based in absurdity of plot, and also, by convention, in stylized action and stock characters, and in physical pranks and punishments that evoke laughter instead of pity. Shrew-ish wives, feckless husbands, flirtatious courtesans, and slaves constantly quarreling with their masters were all the stuff of Plautus, and particularly of his *Menaechmi*, one of his most popular plays with Elizabethans and one which has so much in common with *The Comedy of Errors* that *Menaechmi* is regarded as a source for Shakespeare's play. In *Menaechmi*, two twins are sepa-rated at birth and when one later arrives at the home of the other in Epidamnus, many of the people the stranger encounters—including his twin's wife and servant, a courtesan, and a mountebank pretending to be a doctor —confuse the two men. Both plays center on the wrong twin coming to dinner and on a gold chain meant for the wife given in retaliation to the courtesan; but in the end, Plautus's twins are so enamored of each other—rather like Shakespeare's Dromios at the end of his play—that they decide to travel together and they auction off all the goods of the twin in Epidamnus, including his wife! In each work, the reductive, mechanical quality of events leads to a shameless series of unlikely coincidences, thus supplying a certain mathematical economy of plot. But in Shakespeare's play alone, the twin Antipholuses are given twin Dromios, troping an extended crisscrossing (or chiasmus, according to the popular rhetorical handbook of the period by George Puttenham) in which the strangers and aliens from Syracuse get a wife, a dinner, and a warm welcome, and the inhabitant twins of Ephesus are made strangers and aliens who are abused, exorcised, and punished.

Since appearance alone is what counts in these plays, in Shakespeare as in Plautus, individual identification or personality is usually eradicated, at least until the final scenes.[1] Characters are governed by a single trait so that they appear quite one-dimensional; Plautine (and Shakespearean) farce thus draws upon the Greek notion of *character*, according to which superhuman forces stamp and direct human behavior in a singular and predictable way.[2] For the Elizabethans, too, social and family relationships often dictated behavior rather than individual choice or talent. Luciana's advice to her sister Adriana concerning marriage (2.1.15–25) and to Antipholus of Syracuse (3.2.1–30), echoing almost verbatim conventional sermons of the time, is a reliable index to the Elizabethan culture for which Shakespeare was writing. But this was also a culture at the beginning of transition, and many current social historians of the period now argue that with a shifting economy—from the fixed duties in feudalism to the more fluid ones in a nascent capitalism—many men and especially women were beginning to become aware of what might set them apart in a shifting and competitive world.[3] Centuries before Freud—in characters like Hamlet or Othello or Macbeth or even like Romeo or Juliet—individual consciousness was given emphasis.

Thus recent critics writing in our own time are more keenly concerned with the psychological consequences of a play in which one brother seeking his twin finds himself in a land which is baffling and even threatening. Ruth Nevo, for instance, has written that "If it were not so funny, Shakespeare's first comedy would read like a schizophrenic nightmare: identities are lost, split, engulfed, hallucinated, imploded. Apparently solid citizens (solid at least to themselves) suffer 'ontological uncertainty' in acute forms, wandering about unrecognized by all they encounter."[4] Their individuality, their very selves, are denied them because they fail to arouse the recognition or confirmation in others that we all use for self-identity. Antipholus of Syracuse is warmly received in a strange city; Antipholus of Ephesus is locked out of his own home by his wife, who refuses to acknowledge that he is her husband. Dromio of Syracuse describes the kitchen wench to his master in a way that depersonalizes and deconstructs her, making her nothing more than a global map full of stereotypical prejudices of the day (3.2.97–153). Her explicit grotesqueness sketches in a concentrated way the grotesque events that characterize the play, just as Egeon's initial sense of estrangement is in due course shared by more and more characters. The puzzling, fragmented world they sense—using the best of their logic only to be defeated by illogical occurrences and responses— eliminates the force of reason, while the pressure of the unexpected robs them of any integrated consciousness. The characters of *The Comedy of Errors* become not subjects but objects: integers moved by events and by the playwright, like so many chess pieces on a comic chessboard. Rather than feel their concerns, sharing them, we laugh at them.

In a very real sense, then, such depersonalized characters become comic commodities whose purpose, in a metatheatrical expansion of the market setting, is their commercial value as figures of fun. This is, I think, a way in which all of the matters we have been discussing— comic confusion, farcically endless improbabilities, loss of personal freedom and identity—come together. As recent economic historians have demonstrated, the Elizabethan age, in which individualism was just beginning to be awakened, was an age deeply concerned with a new sense of the market and of the marketability of goods, of talents, and even of people.[5] "The Prince with his subjects," one of Shakespeare's contemporaries writes, "the Master with his servants, one friend and acquaintance with another, the Captain with his soldiers, the Husband and his wife, Women with and among themselves, and, in a word, all the world hoppeth and changeth, runneth and raveth after Marts, Markets, and Merchandising so that all things come into Commerce and pass into Traffic (in a manner) in all times and in all places."[6] While Shakespeare sets the story in Ephesus, the play, performed in London, takes on the features of London itself—the city of trade, the port for sea voyages. One foreigner visiting England in 1592 writes:

London is a large, excellent and mighty city of business, and the most important in the whole kingdom; most of the inhabitants are employed in buying and selling merchandise, and trading in almost every corner of the world, since the river is most useful and convenient for this purpose, considering that ships from France, the Netherlands, Sweden, Denmark, Hamburg and other kingdoms, come almost up to the city, to which they convey goods and receive and take away others in exchange.[7]

Another visitor, in 1617, points out that houses in London are "being all built inward, [so] that the whole room towards the streets may be reserved for shops of tradesmen."[8] Seeing a performance of *The Comedy of Errors* must have caused many in Shakespeare's first (London) audience to be keenly aware of similarities between London's own sea traffic and trade and that which brings strangers ashore in Shakespeare's Ephesus; and Ephesian characters like the goldsmith Angelo, the merchant Balthasar, and the several unnamed merchants might have stepped from the streets outside the theater onto the stage. London guilds in this period, like the guild of goldsmiths or of merchant tailors, controlled the city government as well as its economy, and Steve Rappaport's study of these guilds shows that they grew astonishingly during this period; the Merchant Tailors' Guild alone numbered 2,673 freemen.

Such a commercial revolution must have had a pronounced effect. The "property fetish" that has been seen as the basis of English common law in the period suggests that the gold chain that is disputed in *The Comedy of Errors* was just the sort of acquisition that Londoners themselves focused on; both identity and status depended increasingly on one's material goods. Because the society was more and more cognizant that what one *was* was largely determined by what one *owned*, the chief emphasis in *The Comedy of Errors* on possessions, on being possessed (by marriage, witchcraft, or grace), and on being dispossessed unites the play's Ephesus with Shakespeare's London. The dramatist Thomas Dekker even likens the poet's playhouse to the Royal Exchange, a place of trade in central London: "The Theater is your Poets Royal-Exchange, upon which their Muses (that are now turned to Merchants) meeting, barter away that light commodity of words."[9]

In the earlier part of the sixteenth century, plays were usually staged in the market squares of towns and villages throughout England; what changes in Shakespeare's time is that the market has become the setting and even the theme of plays. The business of *The Comedy of Errors* is business. Many of the speeches are about the exchange of money or property; personal relationships are figured in financial terms. Plautus's Roman market of Epidamnus is changed to Shakespeare's bustling Mediterranean seaport of Ephesus. Additional merchants are added to the cast. Every character in the play has some good or service to sell or trade. Credit and value are central to thought and conversation. (The word *gold* and its compounds occur thirty times, far more than in any other Shakespeare play.) Gold objects and gold pieces—chains and rings, ducats, marks, guilders, and angels—are the chief props of the play.

There is little in *The Comedy of Errors* that resembles Jean-Christophe Agnew's characterization of feudal economy as based on use-value. (In an economy based on use-value, one pays money or invests in goods that are used and used up.) There is much in the play, however, that matches the economy that Agnew identifies as emergent in early modern Europe, an economy based on exchange-value—an economy, that is, in which one exchanged something for something else, such as a penny for admission to a play.[10] This new economy may be caught explicitly in the frequent exchanges of the Antipholuses and their Dromios, in Adriana as wife first to one Antipholus and then, by error, to the other. Materialism informs the premises of the play and commerce its actions. As a playwright, Shakespeare, too, is materialistic and commercial; he capitalizes on Plautus's *Menaechmi,* taught to schoolboys, changing their Latin-grammar-school text into his own dramatic property. Even the title may warn us of this transaction: in the play, *error* moves beyond merely mistake to take on the financial overtones of miscalculation.

*The Comedy of Errors* begins with a merchant who has neglected his duties as a husband and father to attend to his commercial ventures, guilty of leaving a pregnant wife to attend to business. Duke Solinus, in fact, addresses Egeon by his apparent occupation rather than by name:

> Merchant of Syracusa, plead no more.
> I am not partial to infringe our laws.
> The enmity and discord which of late
> Sprung from the rancorous outrage of your duke
> To merchants, our well-dealing countrymen,
> Who, wanting guilders to redeem their lives,
> Have sealed his rigorous statutes with their bloods,
> Excludes all pity from our threat'ning looks.
>                                          (1.1.3–10)

At just the point when he tries to take up the responsibilities of husband and father, Egeon is arrested as a merchant arriving at a forbidden port. He is made the victim of an unexplained trade war. Even so, if he can find enough money, he can buy his freedom (21–24). What at first seems a story about a father seeking his lost son becomes a financial account in which the overriding mercantile system commodifies an individual. Agnew cites Marx as the economic historian who first identified the late sixteenth century as the era when money became a liquid medium with the power "to split the exchange transaction into two mutually indifferent acts: exchange of commodities for money, exchange of money for commodities; purchase and sale."[11] Putting a price on Egeon's life extends and complicates the idea and power of business transactions in the trafficking of the Elizabethan age.

The second scene also begins with a merchant, this time a businessman of Ephesus instructing Antipholus of Syracuse, newly arrived in town, how to protect his property: "Therefore give out you are of Epidamium, / Lest that your goods too soon be confiscate" (1.2.1–2). Antipholus obeys, sending Dromio with his thousand marks—just the amount Egeon is searching for, linking the merchant and the money—to an inn, a place of business called the Centaur. But this friendly merchant will do no more for the stranger, declining to eat with him: "I am invited, sir, to certain merchants," he says, putting investments in money before investments in friendship; "My present business calls me from you now" (1.2.24, 29). Almost at once Dromio of Ephesus appears; it is the first moment of mistaken identity. But recognition of "his" servant is not what provokes Antipholus of Syracuse; rather, "Where have you left the money that I gave you?" he asks (54). When Dromio pleads ignorance, Antipholus becomes agitated and beats him. After Dromio has fled, Antipholus grows more certain of Dromio's guilt—"The villain is o'erraught of all my money" (99)—and more anxious about his own well-being, being dispossessed—"They say this town is full of cozenage" (100). The first act ends with Antipholus's wail: "I greatly fear my money is not safe" (108).

The style in which Dromio of Ephesus reports his encounter with Antipholus of Syracuse ridicules Antipholus's obsession with gold:

When I desired him to come home to dinner,
He asked me for a thousand marks in gold.
"'Tis dinnertime," quoth I. "My gold," quoth he.
"Your meat doth burn," quoth I. "My gold," quoth he.
"Will you come?" quoth I. "My gold," quoth he.
"Where is the thousand marks I gave thee, villain?"
"The pig," quoth I, "is burned." "My gold," quoth he.
                                          (2.1.62–70)

Adriana, though, shares this obsession; once Dromio has left, she tells her sister of her own interest in gold—"he promised me a chain," she says of Antipholus of Ephesus (111) and then compares herself to worn and tarnished gold that has lost its market value:

I see the jewel best enamelèd
Will lose his beauty. Yet the gold bides still
That others touch, and often touching will
Wear gold; yet no man that hath a name
By falsehood and corruption doth it shame.
                                          (114–18)

Her remarks are prescient. In the following act, her husband, returning home late and anxious about his wife's reproaches, asks yet another merchant, the goldsmith Angelo, to excuse his lateness by explaining that Antipholus has been seeing to Angelo's manufacture of a necklace for Antipholus's wife. But Antipholus is treated so badly once he arrives home, being locked out of his house and kept from his dinner, that he takes revenge through other property. Jewelry becomes not a gift of love but a means of punishment. He says to the goldsmith Angelo,

> Get you home
> And fetch the chain; by this, I know, 'tis made.
> Bring it, I pray you, to the Porpentine,
> For there's the house. That chain will I bestow—
> Be it for nothing but to spite my wife—
> Upon mine hostess there. Good sir, make haste.
> Since mine own doors refuse to entertain me,
> I'll knock elsewhere, to see if they'll disdain me.
>                                     (3.1.163–70)

Personal relationships for Antipholus of Ephesus are inevitably business transactions too.

Traditionally, the climax of an Elizabethan comedy occurs in Act 3, but in this play on commodity exchange and capital gains, Act 4 raises the ante with further confusion. Angelo, we learn, is in debt to a merchant about to sail to Persia who needs guilders for his voyage (4.1.4) and, called to account, he turns for credit to his debtor for the chain, Antipholus of Ephesus:

> Saving your merry humor, here's the note
> How much your chain weighs to the utmost carat,
> The fineness of the gold, and chargeful fashion,
> Which doth amount to three-odd ducats more
> Than I stand debted to this gentleman.
> I pray you, see him presently discharged,
> For he is bound to sea, and stays but for it.
>                                     (27–33)

Since it is his twin who has the chain, Antipholus of Ephesus resists, and Angelo has him arrested. Dispossessed of the gold chain, Antipholus of Ephesus is now dispossessed of his freedom, and he sends his Dromio home to fetch ransom money. In the parallel scene that follows, Antipholus of Syracuse, suddenly possessed of the chain, refuses to give it to the courtesan, who expects this pledge of payment and who, in turn, demands from Antipholus of Syracuse the ring she gave to Antipholus of Ephesus. When the Syracusan refuses once more, she condemns him to her court of appeals, Adriana. Here too personal pledges are measured in property.

The transactions that the characters in *The Comedy of Errors* attempt to make, then—their investments, pledges, purchases, and savings—are always susceptible to change. Antipholus of Syracuse is the first to be made aware of this in his sense of instability and incompleteness without his twin:

> He that commends me to mine own content
> Commends me to the thing I cannot get.
> I to the world am like a drop of water
> That in the ocean seeks another drop,
> Who, falling there to find his fellow forth,
> Unseen, inquisitive, confounds himself.
> So I, to find a mother and a brother,
> In quest of them, unhappy, lose myself.
>                                         (1.2.33–40)

It is a short route—just one conversation with the wrong Dromio—from his loss of family (which money cannot buy) to a perceived threat to his individual identity:

They say this town is full of cozenage,
As nimble jugglers that deceive the eye,
Dark-working sorcerers that change the mind,
Soul-killing witches that deform the body,
Disguisèd cheaters, prating mountebanks,
And many suchlike liberties of sin.

(1.2.100–5)[12]

But both of these speeches are soliloquies—moments of internal self-reflection in which Antipholus of Syracuse addresses only himself. It may be important to note that Antipholus of Syracuse is the only character in the play who has soliloquies. This is partly because from the first he is alien to the commercial world of Ephesus and the merchant world of his father. These and his later soliloquies (2.2.225–29; 3.2.173–81; 4.3.1–11), scattered rather evenly as a countermelody to the dominant song of capitalism, allow him to achieve the kind of self-consciousness that we have already seen social historians locating precisely in this period of swiftly developing capitalism.

There is a sense in which such a self-consciousness is aware of danger and prompted by interrogations of events and comments that turn the liquidity of human experience into an understanding of—if not an actual appreciation for—wonder and mystery. Confronted by the gift of a dinner prepared by Adriana, the friendship of Luciana, and the gold chain, Antipholus of Syracuse is open to the opportunities life may afford him; having secured material goods without asking, what he seeks is that which surpasses the material. By no longer wishing to possess goods or people, he earns self-possession. By contrast, the other self-conscious character in *The Comedy of Errors*, Luciana, is more socially conscious, and her self-consciousness rests on communal conventions she would uphold, both in telling Adriana the bases of a successful marriage (2.1.15–25) and in telling Antipholus of Syracuse the need for preserving custom (3.2.1–30). Just as Antipholus of Syracuse in his soliloquies provides a new meaning for use-value—how to use experience for self-education—so Luciana finds a new meaning for exchange-value—the purpose and advantages of counsel.

In Shakespeare's day, as in our own, tragedy pitted men and women against fate (*Romeo and Juliet*) or character (*Macbeth*), while comedy looked at the relationships of people—at families, kinship patterns, friends, communities. What seems to begin as a tragedy in *The Comedy of Errors* is disrupted into farce by inconsistency and confusion, but the strong undertow in the play is toward restoration, reconciliation, and reunion. The apparent strength of this movement toward a comic ending may be an effect of the play's comparative brevity and its severely unified setting. Perhaps because the play is Shakespeare's most economical drama and because here as almost nowhere else save *The Tempest* Shakespeare is concerned with the unity of time, place, and action, *The Comedy of Errors* seems to move inexorably toward a kind of closure despite the heightened and disruptive confusions. Beginning with the search for family, which Egeon gives to Duke Solinus as the reason for his present journey, and with the inner thoughts of pilgrimage, which Antipholus of Syracuse speaks only to himself, the play presents a yearning for wholeness, completeness, that only the reunited family at the end can satisfy. The pronounced effect that the reunion of Egeon's family has on Solinus is testimony to the importance of family integration. So too is the urgency of the Abbess's public admonition of Adriana (5.1.70–89), combined with her confession that she too must rely finally on "wholesome syrups, drugs, and holy prayers, / To make of him a formal man again" (108–9). We seem to have moved into another level of existence altogether, one informed by trust and belief.

But Shakespeare has a way of confusing and complicating the ends of his plays as well as their beginnings. Here it takes more than the wonder and grace of the twins' recognition of each other, or of a reunited family, to resolve all of the play's difficulties. Following the unwinding of misconceptions that have come forth as fast and easily as puns from a Dromio (1.2.62–68), Antipholus of Ephesus attempts a last financial act, an exchange of property ("These ducats pawn I for my father here," 5.1.402). The final power of the play seems to rest with capitalism. But then Solinus frees Egeon at no cost, as a free gesture. Even so, the force of the marketplace extends beyond the play. In rejoining her family, Emilia gives up her long life of service to the priory for a secular existence with her family. Forsaking the vows and life of an abbess, she (together with the play) reenters the world of commerce and of property. Indeed, the merchant's family may make a return voyage to Syracuse, encountering once more the sea of fortune.

---

1. A modern version which follows the plot but uses only one of Shakespeare's actual lines is Rodgers and Hart's musical *The Boys from Syracuse,* with a book by George Abbott. The play opened in November 1938 on Broadway and ran 235 performances; a revival twenty-five years later ran 500 performances. It is preserved on two CDs: Sony SK 53329 and Angel USA ZDM 7 64695 2.

2. Related meanings for the word *character* are "engrave, imprint, or inscribe" as in the character of a person's handwriting, or "instrument for marking, impress." See Jonathan Goldberg, *Writing Matter: From the Hands of the English Renaissance* (Stanford: Stanford University Press, 1990), pp. 24ff. Goldberg draws specifically on Jacques Derrida's *Of Grammatology*, trans. Gayatri Chakravorty Spivak (Baltimore: Johns Hopkins University Press, 1976).

3. The seminal text is *A History of Private Life*, gen. eds. Philippe Ariès and Georges Duby, 2 vols. (Cambridge, Mass.: Harvard University Press, 1988).

4. Ruth Nevo, *Comic Transformations in Shakespeare* (New York: Methuen, 1980), p. 22.

5. See, for example, Jean-Christophe Agnew, *Worlds Apart: The Market and the Theater in Anglo-American Thought, 1550–1750* (Cambridge: Cambridge University Press, 1986); Ian W. Archer, *The Pursuit of Stability: Social Relations in Elizabethan London* (Cambridge: Cambridge University Press, 1991); and Steve Rappaport, *Worlds Within Worlds: Structures of Life in Sixteenth-Century London* (Cambridge: Cambridge University Press, 1989).

6. John Wheeler, *A Treatise of Commerce: Wherein Are Shewed the Commodities Arising by a Wel Ordered, and Rvled Trade, Such as that of the Societie of Merchantes Adventurers* (1601), sig. B2.

7. Frederick, duke of Würtenberg in 1592 as quoted in F. P. Wilson, *Life in Shakespeare's England* (Cambridge: Cambridge University Press, 1939), p. 84.

8. Fynes Moryson, *Itinerary* (1617), quoted in Wilson, *Life in Shakespeare's England*, p. 85.

9. Thomas Dekker, *The Guls Horne-booke* (1609), sig. E2.

10. See Agnew, *Worlds Apart,* p. 53.

11. Ibid., p. 43.

12. The psychological effect of this passage is analyzed by Coppélia Kahn in *Man's Estate: Masculine Identity in Shakespeare* (Berkeley: University of California Press, 1981), pp. 200–5.

# Further Reading

## The Comedy of Errors

Arthos, John. "Shakespeare's Transformation of Plautus." *Comparative Drama* 1 (1967–68): 239–53. Revised and reprinted in *Shakespeare: The Early Writings*, pp. 8–41. London: Bowes & Bowes; Totowa, N.J.: Rowman & Littlefield, 1972.

In adapting the *Menaechmi*, Shakespeare, Arthos claims, was attracted to features in the works of Plautus (exuberance, musicality, and elements of romance and the fantastic) that he could refashion, "extending their function and significance" to yield a comic vision more golden than hard-edged. Shakespeare emphasized a "yearning for the absolute" (the defining note of the romance genre) and thus transformed a comic world in which conflict is the norm into one that values communion on multiple levels.

Barber, C. L., and Richard P. Wheeler. "Domestic Comedy." In *The Whole Journey: Shakespeare's Power of Development*, pp. 67–85. Berkeley: University of California Press, 1986.

Emphasizing the strategies of splitting and displacement, Barber and Wheeler's psychoanalytic reading of this early play "about family bonds" argues that the two Antipholuses derive in part from Shakespeare's own felt division between being a married man in Stratford and a playwright in London who is also estranged from his once-prosperous father, now fallen on hard times. The play works to merge these roles into a reunited family. "As within the fiction the twins refind the intact family,

Shakespeare refinds it by having made the fiction." (The first part of the essay reprints Barber's "Shakespearian Comedy in *The Comedy of Errors*" [*College English* 25 (1964): 493–97], in which the author praises the play's verbal energy, the replacement of Plautus's "fractions of human nature" with characters "conceived as whole people," and Shakespeare's prolific use of domestic detail which "feed[s] Elizabethan life into the mill of Roman farce.")

Brooks, Harold. "Themes and Structures in *The Comedy of Errors*." In *Early Shakespeare*, edited by John Russell Brown and Bernard Harris, pp. 54–71. London: Edward Arnold, 1961.

In this frequently cited essay, Brooks examines events, characters, themes (e.g., relationship, cosmic order, and the dangers of illusion), and imagery (particularly animal and water images) to arrive at the "great value" of "the harmonic structure: the structure which by parallel, contrast, or cross-reference . . . makes us compare one passage or person of the play with another, and so find an enriched significance in both." Act 1, scene 2 serves as a model for establishing the play's architectural artistry, Shakespeare's command of scenic units, his ability to pay constant attention to past, present, and future action, and his talent for "combinative power" in composing a play "of diverse yet cooperating strands and tones."

Church of England. "Homily on Obedience." In *Elizabethan Backgrounds*, edited by Arthur F. Kinney, pp. 60–70. Hamden: Archon Books, 1975; reprinted 1990.

The primary sermon read monthly at services in all English parish churches is cited by Luciana in 2.1 to establish basic values tested in the play. As Kinney points out in his introductory comments (pp. 44–48), this homily "is perhaps the chief repository of common-place Elizabethan [analogical] thought and belief [especially the doctrine of order and degree]." Kinney's text is taken from the first Elizabethan edition of *Certayne Sermons or Homilies* (1559), which went through ten subsequent editions by 1595.

Freedman, Barbara. "Egeon's Debt: Self-Division and Self-Redemption in *The Comedy of Errors.*" *English Literary Renaissance* 10 (1980): 360–83.

Using a psychoanalytic approach to solve a central problem in *Errors* scholarship—namely, the inability of critics "to prove the frame plot intrinsic to the play or the main plot purposive"—Freedman reads the farcical business involving the twin Antipholuses as the means by which the divided Egeon (one son corresponding to the marital, guilt-ridden side of the father's psyche, and the other to his single, wandering side) ultimately achieves unity and redemption. Thus interpreted, *Errors* "no longer appears to be a random and senseless farce of mistaken identities, but a carefully orchestrated psychological drama in which dissociated parts of the self are meaningfully united." In a later, denser reading, Freedman draws on Freud's sense of the uncanny, the unfamiliar familiar, to suggest that any attempt to unify the ego results in frustration and defeat, and any attempt to unify the plot of this play will prove impossible. See "Reading Errantly: Misrecognition and the Uncanny in *The Comedy of Errors,*" in *Staging the Gaze: Postmodernism, Psychoanalysis, and Shakespearean Comedy,* pp. 78–113 (Ithaca: Cornell University Press, 1991).

Grennan, Eamon. "Arm and Sleeve: Nature and Custom in *The Comedy of Errors.*" *Philological Quarterly* 59 (1980): 150–64.

Grennan finds the play centered in the conflict between physical nature and social custom, experience, and expectation. He traces this dialectic from the emblematic first scene through the intensifying "natural" frenzy of the fourth act, which necessitates the strict conventionality of the law, to the final synthesis achieved in the person of the Abbess, "the perfect fusion of nature (mother) and custom (nun)."

Hennings, Thomas P. "The Anglican Doctrine of the Affectionate Marriage in *The Comedy of Errors.*" *Modern Language Quarterly* 47 (1986): 91–107.
    Hennings uses the "Homily on the State of Matrimony," a frequently read sermon, along with marriage manuals of the time, to demonstrate that *Errors* "is not so much an imitation of the *Menaechmi* as it is a deliberate Christian corrective of the Latin play and its Saturnalian themes." Citing Adriana's exchange with her sister at the beginning of 2.1 and her encounter with the wrong Antipholus in the second half of 2.2, Hennings makes the case for Adriana, not Luciana, as the better spokesperson for Anglican teaching on spousal friendship and intimacy, marital duties of both partners, and the wrongness of the double standard. Like Adriana, the Abbess's voice also supports the Anglican doctrine of conjugal affection. This sermon, and the "Homily on Obedience," which also informs the play, can be found in the 1968 reprint of the 1623 edition of *Certaine Sermons or Homilies,* edited by Mary Ellen Rickey and Thomas B. Stroup (Gainesville, Fla.: Scholars' Facsimiles and Reprints).

Homan, Sidney. "*The Comedy of Errors:* 'And here we wander in illusions.'" In *Shakespeare's Theater of Presence: Language, Spectacle and the Audience,* pp. 31–45. Lewisburg: Bucknell University Press, 1986.
    Writing as a theater director, Homan describes the

effect of staging the play from the viewpoint of those in it and those who watch it and finds both groups engaged in a similar sense of theatricality. "Given the improbabilities of its plot, what engages us in *Errors* is not so much its mirror image of normal life but rather the gap in Shakespeare's theater of presence between our sense of the play's purpose and the perceptions of its characters, who, until the very end, have no sense of their own play on that same stage we witness both aurally and visually." In the final scene, both characters and audience "see the events of the day *as* illusions, as *theater*, as comic errors in a comedy of errors."

Huston, J. Dennis. "Playing with Discontinuity: Mistakings and Mistimings in *The Comedy of Errors*." In *Shakespeare's Comedies of Play*, pp. 14–34. New York: Columbia University Press, 1981.

In this postmodernist reading of *Errors*, Huston likens the play to a puppet show in spirit, locating its considerable power in radical discontinuities which readers and playgoers liken to the discontinuity and fragmentation of all human experience. Huston pays special attention to the "misleading beginning" (i.e., the disparity between the pathos of Egeon's plight and the audience's expectation of a "comedy of errors"), to Emilia's surprise revelation, and to examples of "discontinuous behavior" in between.

Kehler, Dorothea. "Shakespeare's Emilias and the Politics of Celibacy." In *In Another Country: Feminist Perspectives on Renaissance Drama*, edited by Kehler and Susan Baker, pp. 157–78, esp. pp. 159–61. Metuchen, N.J.: Scarecrow Press, 1991.

Kehler is concerned with the "ideological function" of the Abbess (Emilia) within the patriarchal society of the play. Her actions and authority interrogate

Luciana's position in 2.1, but her own celibacy, neither wife nor widow, is also an "error" which confounds gender roles and shows the irreducible inadequacies in the social formation shared by the first playgoers with the characters in the play. Emilia is successful in wielding power because of her ambiguous state as *woman*, her celibacy and age "dissipat[ing] the threat of [her] sexuality" and empowering her to move from a marginal position to one of authority.

Kinney, Arthur F. "Shakespeare's *Comedy of Errors* and the Nature of Kinds." *Studies in Philology* 85 (1988): 29–52.

Exploring how *Errors* "redefine[s] the nature of kinds," Kinney contends that the Plautine farce Shakespeare knew at grammar school is joined to the mystery plays he saw as a boy. The lessons on "reuniting" and losing oneself to find a fuller self, when taken with the more frequently noted passages on order, marriage, and the parent-child relationship, make Paul's letter to the Ephesians "the source that inspired *all* parts of *Errors*."

Knapp, Margaret, and Michal Kobialka. "Shakespeare and the Prince of Purpoole: The 1594 Production of *The Comedy of Errors* at Gray's Inn Hall." *Theatre History Studies* 4 (1984): 70–81.

This is the fullest investigation into the occasion of the 1594 performance of *Errors*—the first recorded performance—during the Christmas Revels at Gray's Inn. The presiding figure was the Prince of Purpoole (a corruption of Portpool, the London parish in which Gray's Inn was located). Drawing upon the account found in the *Gesta Grayorum* and measurements of the theatrical space, the authors reconstruct the staging and provide a chronological table of the many celebrations held between December 20 and Shrove Tuesday, thereby showing that the performance of *Errors* was only one enter-tainment among several on December 28.

Lanier, Douglas. "'Stigmatical in Making': The Material Character of *The Comedy of Errors*." *English Literary Renaissance* 23 (1993): 81–112.

In this material analysis, Lanier sees *Errors* as the crafting of things—of gestures, postures, sounds, and costumes which call attention to their own illogicality and theatricality. Through its copious disruptions of "identity-effects," *Errors* interrogates and subverts the cultural assumption that "who you see is who you got." Attention to the play's pervasive corporeality and the materialist premises of its commercial world helps rescue *Errors* from the damning "marginality" of farce.

McDonald, Russ. "Fear of Farce." In *"Bad" Shakespeare: Revaluations of the Shakespeare Canon*, edited by Maurice Charney, pp. 77–90. Rutherford, N.J.: Fairleigh Dickinson University Press, 1988.

McDonald defends *Errors* as an outright farce in which Shakespeare, rather than finding the form embarrassing, uses it to provide what comedy and other forms cannot: "the production of ideas through rowdy action, the pleasures of 'non-significant' wordplay, freedom from the limits of credibility, mental exercise induced by the rapid tempo of the action, unrestricted laughter —the satisfactions of various kinds of extravagance." As farce, the emphasis is on "the delights of disjunction," but as comedy, the play "moves toward a restoration of human ties and the formation of new ones."

Parker, Patricia. "Elder and Younger: The Opening Scene of *The Comedy of Errors*." *Shakespeare Quarterly* 34 (1983): 325–27.

Parker defends the seeming confusion of elder and

younger twins in Egeon's account of the family's shipwreck (1.1.62–93) as logical and consistent, not an example of authorial nodding. The key to unlocking the editorial crux in "My youngest boy, and yet my eldest care" (1.124) is found in the rhetorical crossing (chiasmus) of "youngest boy" and "eldest care"—also present in the crucial line "Fixing our eyes on whom our care was fixed" (84). The prominence of "crossing" in 1.1 suggests a pattern of exchange within "the larger allusive structure of the play as a whole."

Plautus. *The Manaechmus Twins and Other Plays*, translated by Lionel Casson. New York: W. W. Norton, 1971.
   This accessible modern translation of the Plautine farce, the *Menaechmi*, Shakespeare's primary source, shows the elements on which *The Comedy of Errors* was built—a wandering twin and a twin whose marriage is interrupted by a gold chain and a courtesan and the confusion of two men. *Errors* also has similarities with Plautus's *Amphitruo* (where a wife locks out her husband) and his *Rudens* (which combines farce and romance). William Warner's translation of the *Menaechmi* (1595), published a year after Shakespeare's play, is reprinted in *Narrative and Dramatic Sources in Shakespeare,* edited by Geoffrey Bullough, 1:12–39; scenes from the *Amphitruo* follow (New York: Columbia University Press, 1966).

Salgādo, Gāmini. "'Time's Deformed Hand': Sequence, Consequence, and Inconsequence in *The Comedy of Errors.*" *Shakespeare Survey* 25 (1972): 81–91.
   A recollection of the dominant and rapidly ticking clock in Komisarjevsky's 1938 *Errors* at Stratford-upon-Avon introduces Salgādo's discussion of "the movement of time and its apparent aberrations" in the play. Disruptions of normally accepted temporal and causal se-

quences are responsible for the comic "horror" of confusion and loss of identity. The "most explicit statement" of the play's preoccupation with the "divergence" of public and private time (clock time vs. inward time) is found in 4.2.66: "The hours come back. That did I never hear." Salgādo finds more references to clock time in *Errors* than in any other Shakespearean comedy.

Slights, Camille Wells. "Egeon's Friends and Relations: *The Comedy of Errors.*" In *Shakespeare's Comic Commonwealths*, pp. 13–31. Toronto: University of Toronto Press, 1993.

Slights claims that the play is less concerned with testing "individual character in adversity" than in "shared social structures" in which "reality becomes [intelligible]." She sees the play upholding not so much family as communal values. The play's humor derives largely from the characters' dependence on social relations and a threatened loss of their social roles as husband, wife, servant; as a result, "all the major characters undergo the Kafkaesque experience of suddenly finding themselves in a nightmare world of strange transformations and inexplicable events." *Errors* "emphasizes the need to belong to society, not the need to reform it."

Tetzeli von Rosador, Kurt. "Plotting the Early Comedies: *The Comedy of Errors, Love's Labour's Lost, The Two Gentlemen of Verona.*" *Shakespeare Survey* 37 (1984): 13–22, esp. pp. 14–17.

Advocating a return to an idea of plot derived and adapted from Aristotle and the Terentian theorists, the author focuses on plot's thematic dimension and "inexorable forward movement," using 1.1 to illustrate the play's central pattern of oscillation between danger and evasion. Crucial to the pattern of building up and then

postponing danger is Shakespeare's tripartite construction of scenes: "the opening section of each may drama-
tize the conditions which give rise to danger or violence,
the middle their imminent or actual outbreak, the last
their evasion and the establishment of a new, precarious
balance."

Truax, Elizabeth. "The Metamorphosis of Heroes and
Monsters in *The Comedy of Errors.*" In *Metamorphosis in
Shakespeare's Plays: A Pageant of Heroes, Gods, Maids
and Monsters*, pp. 28–53. Lewiston: Edwin Mellen Press,
1992.
    Using folklore, romances, iconographic dictionaries,
and emblem books popular in Shakespeare's day, Truax
proposes that commonplace animal lore and current
ideas about metamorphosis (drawn from Ovid) are
central to appreciating *Errors*, giving it depth and making it more than a "stage-joke." Truax provides extensive
commentary on the symbolically fitting nomenclature
of inns (the Centaur, Porpentine, and Tiger) and places
of residence (the Phoenix) designated in the play. The
absence of apparent sources for the names of the inns
suggests their linkage "with the implicit theme of the
play—men who act like animals do, in a sense, become
them." The reference to the phoenix, on the other hand,
is appropriate to the imagery of death and resurrection
that is "implicit" in much of the dramatic action.

Wood, Robert E. "Cooling the Comedy: Television as a
Medium for Shakespeare's *Comedy of Errors.*" *Litera-
ture/Film Quarterly* 14 (1986): 195–202.
    Wood argues that the 1983 BBC-TV/Time-Life pro-
duction of *Errors*, a "successful marriage" of text to
medium, reveals the strengths both of Shakespeare's
play and of contemporary television as a way of understanding its comic relationships and "characteristics

unique to the theme of twins." Wood emphasizes the production's consistent evoking of intimacy by way of the close-up: since "so much of the play is about being looked at . . . the simple close-up of an actor's face becomes an instrument of power." The techniques of television (split-screen reproduction, multiple camera angles, close-ups, etc.) nicely preserve the "deliberate unreality" that is "the essence of *The Comedy of Errors.*"

## Shakespeare's Language

Abbott, E. A. *A Shakespearian Grammar*. New York: Haskell House, 1972.

This compact reference book, first published in 1870, helps with many difficulties in Shakespeare's language. It systematically accounts for a host of differences between Shakespeare's usage and sentence structure and our own.

Blake, Norman. *Shakespeare's Language: An Introduction*. New York: St. Martin's Press, 1983.

This general introduction to Elizabethan English discusses various aspects of the language of Shakespeare and his contemporaries, offering possible meanings for hundreds of ambiguous constructions.

Dobson, E. J. *English Pronunciation, 1500–1700*. 2 vols. Oxford: Clarendon Press, 1968.

This long and technical work includes chapters on spelling (and its reformation), phonetics, stressed vowels, and consonants in early modern English.

Houston, John. *Shakespearean Sentences: A Study in Style and Syntax*. Baton Rouge: Louisiana State University Press, 1988.

Houston studies Shakespeare's stylistic choices, considering matters such as sentence length and the relative positions of subject, verb, and direct object. Examining plays throughout the canon in a roughly chronological, developmental order, he analyzes how sentence structure is used in setting tone, in characterization, and for other dramatic purposes.

Onions, C. T. *A Shakespeare Glossary.* Oxford: Clarendon Press, 1986.

This revised edition updates Onions's standard, selective glossary of words and phrases in Shakespeare's plays that are now obsolete, archaic, or obscure.

Partridge, Eric. *Shakespeare's Bawdy.* London: Routledge & Kegan Paul, 1955.

After an introductory essay, "The Sexual, the Homosexual, and Non-Sexual Bawdy in Shakespeare," Partridge provides a comprehensive glossary of "bawdy" phrases and words from the plays.

Robinson, Randal. *Unlocking Shakespeare's Language: Help for the Teacher and Student.* Urbana, Ill.: National Council of Teachers of English and the ERIC Clearinghouse on Reading and Communication Skills, 1989.

Specifically designed for the high-school and undergraduate college teacher and student, Robinson's book addresses the problems that most often hinder present-day readers of Shakespeare. Through work with his own students, Robinson found that many readers today are particularly puzzled by such stylistic devices as subject-verb inversion, interrupted structures, and compression. He shows how our own colloquial language contains comparable structures, and thus helps students recognize such structures when they find them in Shakespeare's plays. This book supplies worksheets—

with examples from major plays—to illuminate and remedy such problems as unusual sequences of words and the separation of related parts of sentences.

## Shakespeare's Life

Baldwin, T. W. *William Shakspere's Petty School.* Urbana: University of Illinois Press, 1943.

Baldwin here investigates the theory and practice of the petty school, the first level of education in Elizabethan England. He focuses on that educational system primarily as it is reflected in Shakespeare's art.

Baldwin, T. W. *William Shakspere's Small Latine and Lesse Greeke.* 2 vols. Urbana: University of Illinois Press, 1944.

Baldwin attacks the view that Shakespeare was an uneducated genius—a view that had been dominant among Shakespeareans since the eighteenth century. Instead, Baldwin shows, the educational system of Shakespeare's time would have given the playwright a strong background in the classics, and there is much in the plays that shows how Shakespeare benefited from such an education.

Beier, A. L., and Roger Finlay, eds. *London 1500–1700: The Making of the Metropolis.* New York: Longman, 1986.

Focusing on the economic and social history of early modern London, these collected essays probe aspects of metropolitan life, including "Population and Disease," "Commerce and Manufacture," and "Society and Change."

Bentley, G. E. *Shakespeare's Life: A Biographical Handbook.* New Haven: Yale University Press, 1961.

This "just-the-facts" account presents the surviving documents of Shakespeare's life against an Elizabethan background.

Chambers, E. K. *William Shakespeare: A Study of Facts and Problems.* 2 vols. Oxford: Clarendon Press, 1930.
Analyzing in great detail the scant historical data, Chambers's complex, scholarly study considers the nature of the texts in which Shakespeare's work is preserved.

Cressy, David. *Education in Tudor and Stuart England.* London: Edward Arnold, 1975.
This volume collects sixteenth-, seventeenth-, and early-eighteenth-century documents detailing aspects of formal education in England, such as the curriculum, the control and organization of education, and the education of women.

Dutton, Richard. *William Shakespeare: A Literary Life.* New York: St. Martin's Press, 1989.
Not a biography in the traditional sense, Dutton's very readable work nevertheless "follows the contours of Shakespeare's life" as he examines Shakespeare's career as playwright and poet, with consideration of his patrons, theatrical associations, and audience.

Fraser, Russell. *Young Shakespeare.* New York: Columbia University Press, 1988.
Fraser focuses on Shakespeare's first thirty years, paying attention simultaneously to his life and art.

De Grazia, Margreta. *Shakespeare Verbatim: The Reproduction of Authenticity and the Apparatus of 1790.* Oxford: Clarendon Press, 1991.
De Grazia traces and discusses the development of

such editorial criteria as authenticity, historical period-ization, factual biography, chronological development, and close reading, locating as the point of origin Edmond Malone's 1790 edition of Shakespeare's works. There are interesting chapters on the First Folio and on the "legendary" versus the "documented" Shakespeare.

Schoenbaum, S. *William Shakespeare: A Compact Documentary Life.* New York: Oxford University Press, 1977.

This standard biography economically presents the essential documents from Shakespeare's time in an accessible narrative account of the playwright's life.

## Shakespeare's Theater

Bentley, G. E. *The Profession of Player in Shakespeare's Time, 1590–1642.* Princeton: Princeton University Press, 1984.

Bentley readably sets forth a wealth of evidence about performance in Shakespeare's time, with special attention to the relations between player and company, and the business of casting, managing, and touring.

Berry, Herbert. *Shakespeare's Playhouses.* New York: AMS Press, 1987.

Berry's six essays collected here discuss (with illustrations) varying aspects of the four playhouses in which Shakespeare had a financial stake: the Theatre in Shoreditch, the Blackfriars, and the first and second Globe.

Cook, Ann Jennalie. *The Privileged Playgoers of Shakespeare's London.* Princeton: Princeton University Press, 1981.

Cook's work argues, on the basis of sociological,

economic, and documentary evidence, that Shakespeare's audience—and the audience for English Renaissance drama generally—consisted mainly of the "privileged."

Greg, W. W. *Dramatic Documents from the Elizabethan Playhouses.* 2 vols. Oxford: Clarendon Press, 1931.

Greg itemizes and briefly describes many of the play manuscripts that survive from the period 1590 to around 1660, including, among other things, players' parts. His second volume offers facsimiles of selected manuscripts.

Gurr, Andrew. *Playgoing in Shakespeare's London.* Cambridge: Cambridge University Press, 1987.

Gurr charts how the theatrical enterprise developed from its modest beginnings in the late 1560s to become a thriving institution in the 1600s. He argues that there were important changes over the period 1567–1644 in the playhouses, the audience, and the plays.

Harbage, Alfred. *Shakespeare's Audience.* New York: Columbia University Press, 1941.

Harbage investigates the fragmentary surviving evidence to interpret the size, composition, and behavior of Shakespeare's audience.

Hattaway, Michael. *Elizabethan Popular Theatre: Plays in Performance.* London: Routledge & Kegan Paul, 1982.

Beginning with a study of the popular drama of the late Elizabethan age—a description of the stages, performance conditions, and acting of the period—this volume concludes with an analysis of five well-known plays of the 1590s, one of them (*Titus Andronicus*) by Shakespeare.

Shapiro, Michael. *Children of the Revels: The Boy Companies of Shakespeare's Time and Their Plays.* New York: Columbia University Press, 1977.
Shapiro chronicles the history of the amateur and quasi-professional child companies that flourished in London at the end of Elizabeth's reign and the beginning of James's.

## The Publication of Shakespeare's Plays

Blayney, Peter. *The First Folio of Shakespeare.* Hanover, Md.: Folger, 1991.
Blayney's accessible account of the printing and later life of the First Folio—an amply illustrated catalog to a 1991 Folger Shakespeare Library exhibition—analyzes the mechanical production of the First Folio, describing how the Folio was made, by whom and for whom, how much it cost, and its ups and downs (or, rather, downs and ups) since its printing in 1623.

Hinman, Charlton. *The Printing and Proof-Reading of the First Folio of Shakespeare.* 2 vols. Oxford: Clarendon Press, 1963.
In the most arduous study of a single book ever undertaken, Hinman attempts to reconstruct how the Shakespeare First Folio of 1623 was set into type and run off the press, sheet by sheet. He also provides almost all the known variations in readings from copy to copy.

Hinman, Charlton. *The Norton Facsimile: The First Folio of Shakespeare.* New York: W. W. Norton, 1968.
This facsimile presents a photographic reproduction of an "ideal" copy of the First Folio of Shakespeare; Hinman attempts to represent each page in its most fully corrected state.

# Key to
# Famous Lines and Phrases

The pleasing punishment that women bear—

[*Egeon*—1.1.46]

. . . we may pity though not pardon thee.

[*Duke*—1.1.97]

To tell sad stories of my own mishaps.

[*Egeon*—1.1.120]

. . . headstrong liberty is lashed with woe.

[*Luciana*—2.1.15]

. . . they say every why hath a wherefore.

[*Dromio of Syracuse*—2.2.45–46]

. . . what he hath scanted men in hair, he hath given
them in wit.        [*Dromio of Syracuse*—2.2.88–89]

Small cheer and great welcome makes a merry feast.

[*Balthasar*—3.1.33–34]

There is something in the wind . . .

[*Antipholus of Ephesus*—3.1.107]

215

. . . we'll pluck a crow together.
                    [*Dromio of Ephesus*—3.1.131–32]

The venom clamors of a jealous woman
Poisons more deadly than a mad dog's tooth.
                    [*Abbess*—5.1.71–72]

# THE FOLGER SHAKESPEARE LIBRARY

The world's leading center for Shakespeare studies presents
acclaimed editions of Shakespeare's plays.

All's Well That Ends Well
Antony and Cleopatra
As You Like It
The Comedy of Errors
Cymbeline
Hamlet
Henry IV, Part 1
Henry IV, Part 2
Henry V
Henry VI, Part 1
Henry VI, Part 2
Henry VI, Part 3
Henry VIII
Julius Caesar
King John
King Lear
Love's Labor's Lost
Macbeth
Measure for Measure
The Merchant of Venice
The Merry Wives of Windsor
A Midsummer Night's Dream

Much Ado About Nothing
Othello
Pericles
Richard II
Richard III
Romeo and Juliet
Shakespeare's Sonnets
Shakespeare's Sonnets
 and Poems
The Taming of the Shrew
The Tempest
Timon of Athens
Titus Andronicus
Troilus and Cressida
Twelfth Night
The Two Gentlemen of Verona
The Winter's Tale
Three Comedies: The Taming
 of the Shrew/A Midsummer
 Night's Dream/Twelfth Night
Three Tragedies: Hamlet/
 Macbeth/Romeo and Juliet

For more information on Folger Shakespeare Library Editions, including
Shakespeare Set Free teaching guides, visit www.simonsays.com.

SIMON & SCHUSTER
PAPERBACKS
A CBS COMPANY